Cambridge Elements ≡

Elements in Earth System Governance
edited by
Frank Biermann
Utrecht University
Aarti Gupta
Wageningen University
Michael Mason
London School of Economics and Political Science

A GREEN AND JUST RECOVERY FROM COVID-19?

Government Investment in the Energy Transition during the Pandemic

Kyla Tienhaara, *Queen's University*
Tom Moerenhout, *International Institute for Sustainable Development*
Vanessa Corkal, *International Institute for Sustainable Development*
Joachim Roth, *International Institute for Sustainable Development*
Hannah Ascough, *Queen's University*
Jessica Herrera Betancur, *Queen's University*
Samantha Hussman, *Queen's University*
Jessica Oliver, *Queen's University*
Kabir Shahani, *Queen's University*
Tianna Tischbein, *Queen's University*

CAMBRIDGE
UNIVERSITY PRESS

Shaftesbury Road, Cambridge CB2 8EA, United Kingdom

One Liberty Plaza, 20th Floor, New York, NY 10006, USA

477 Williamstown Road, Port Melbourne, VIC 3207, Australia

314–321, 3rd Floor, Plot 3, Splendor Forum, Jasola District Centre, New Delhi – 110025, India

103 Penang Road, #05–06/07, Visioncrest Commercial, Singapore 238467

Cambridge University Press is part of Cambridge University Press & Assessment, a department of the University of Cambridge.

We share the University's mission to contribute to society through the pursuit of education, learning and research at the highest international levels of excellence.

www.cambridge.org
Information on this title: www.cambridge.org/9781009462570

DOI: 10.1017/9781009319782

First published 2023

A catalogue record for this publication is available from the British Library

ISBN 978-1-009-46257-0 Hardback
ISBN 978-1-009-31981-2 Paperback
ISSN 2631-7818 (online)
ISSN 2631-780X (print)

Cambridge University Press & Assessment has no responsibility for the persistence or accuracy of URLs for external or third-party internet websites referred to in this publication and does not guarantee that any content on such websites is, or will remain, accurate or appropriate.

A Green and Just Recovery from COVID-19?

Government Investment in the Energy Transition during the Pandemic

Elements in Earth System Governance

DOI: 10.1017/9781009319782
First published online: October 2023

Kyla Tienhaara, *Queen's University*

Tom Moerenhout, *International Institute for Sustainable Development*

Vanessa Corkal, *International Institute for Sustainable Development*

Joachim Roth, *International Institute for Sustainable Development*

Hannah Ascough, *Queen's University*

Jessica Herrera Betancur, *Queen's University*

Samantha Hussman, *Queen's University*

Jessica Oliver, *Queen's University*

Kabir Shahani, *Queen's University*

Tianna Tischbein, *Queen's University*

Author for correspondence: Kyla Tienhaara, kt71@queensu.ca

Abstract: Stimulus spending to address the economic crisis brought on by the COVID-19 pandemic has the potential to either facilitate the transition away from fossil energy or to lock in carbon-intensive technologies and infrastructure for decades to come. Whether they are focused on green sectors or not, stimulus measures can alleviate or reinforce socioeconomic inequality. This Element delves into the data in the Energy Policy Tracker to assess how energy policies adopted during the pandemic will expedite decarbonization and explores whether governments address inequities through policies targeted to disadvantaged, marginalized, and underserved individuals and communities. The overall finding is that the recovery has not been sufficiently green or just. Nevertheless, a small number of policies aim to advance distributive justice and provide potential models for policymakers as they continue to attempt to "build back better." This title is also available as Open Access on Cambridge Core.

Keywords: Climate change, green stimulus, COVID-19, just transition, energy policy

ISBNs: 9781009462570 (HB), 9781009319812 (PB), 9781009319782 (OC)
ISSNs: 2631-7818 (online), 2631-780X (print)

Contents

example, limits on international travel had a dramatic impact on aviation (McKinsey & Company 2022). Reductions in economic activity depressed oil prices, compounding the impacts of earlier economic contractions and price wars and leading to a "scale of the collapse in oil demand . . . [that] is well in excess of the oil industry's capacity to adjust" (IEA 2020c). The reduction in energy demand also caused financial trouble for the coal sector, which was already struggling in many countries before the pandemic (Rowlatt 2020). Although these are industries that need to be rapidly phased-out to keep warming below 1.5°C, a completely unmanaged decline would have devastating impacts for many communities and a destabilizing effect on the global economy.

However, it now appears that these impacts were, by and large, temporary. Emissions began rebounding as soon as the first set of restrictions were eased in the major economies (Harvey 2020). The fossil fuel industry recovered quickly, with coal power generation reaching an all-time high in 2021 (IEA 2021a). Demand for gas rose over 4 percent in 2021, erasing the losses in 2020 (IEA 2022a). While the oil market was considered less likely to return to "normal" post-pandemic (IEA 2021c), prices reached their highest levels in six years even prior to the war in Ukraine, which may increase investment in the sector. The recovery for the airline industry has been slower, but the International Air Transport Association expects the industry to return to profitability in 2023 (Josephs 2021).

In addition to being short-lived, the environmental effects of the restrictions imposed on economic activity were insufficient to address the ecological crisis. Even though emissions were 6.4 percent lower in 2020 than they were in 2019 (Tollefson 2021), this is still less of a drop than the 7.6 percent annual reduction required to meet the Paris Agreement 1.5°C objective (UNEP 2019). In effect, the pandemic starkly illustrated that emissions reductions on the scale required to keep below 1.5°C or even 2°C of warming cannot be induced through behavior changes (like driving less) alone and will require sustained government intervention to facilitate a fundamental transition away from fossil fuel production and consumption, toward low-carbon energy sources.

In this respect, potentially the most important impact of the pandemic is that it created an opportunity for governments to invest in measures that would simultaneously address the economic crisis and accelerate the energy transition. The acknowledgment early on by many economists, governments, and international organizations that substantial government spending would be required not only to keep businesses and individuals afloat during lockdowns but also to stimulate an economic recovery when activity was permitted to resume led to proposals for "green stimulus." In March 2020, a survey of 231 finance ministers, central bank officials, and economists from across the G20 showed substantial support for green stimulus measures such as government spending on clean energy infrastructure (Hepburn et al. 2020). Calls for a "green recovery" and to "build back better" were made by numerous international organizations, including the International Energy Agency (IEA), Organisation for Economic Cooperation and Development (OECD), World Bank, and International Monetary Fund. In late 2020, the EU set a target of 37 percent of its recovery to be focused on a green transition (Taylor 2020).

In addition to the desire to address the climate crisis, experts noted that green stimulus can deliver more "bang for the buck" than traditional carbon-intensive industries, because renewable energy and energy efficiency are very labor-intensive sectors (Pollin et al. 2014, Garrett-Peltier 2017; Pollin and Chakraborty 2020). Green stimulus can also lead to economic savings (through lower energy costs) and spur innovation (Allan et al. 2020). Experts also emphasized that decisions taken in response to the COVID-19 crisis were critical because they would determine the world's development patterns for decades to come. A green recovery was, therefore, not just about investing in green sectors but also about not providing further subsidies to carbon-intensive sectors (Johnson et al. 2020; Sanchez et al. 2021).

1.2 A Just Recovery?

The COVID-19 pandemic both highlighted and exacerbated long-standing health and social inequities across the globe. While this alone would explain why there is a need for the economic recovery to be *just* as well as *green*, it is also increasingly apparent that the ecological crisis is driven by socioeconomic inequalities. In addition to the fact that the richest segments of society are responsible for the largest share of GHGs, wealthy elites also work to obstruct and undermine public support for climate policy through their influence in government and the media (Green and Healy 2022). Thus, in addition to the moral argument that it is "unfair to allow disproportionate burdens to continue to fall on already marginalized groups (current or future), or to suppress their voices and values" (Martin et al. 2020, 20), there are also practical reasons to address social inequality and emissions reductions at the same time. Policy measures will only succeed if the public believes that they are fair and legitimate (Martin et al. 2020). Measures seen as hurting rural communities, the working class, and the poor, such as the fuel taxes in France that sparked the yellow-vest movement, are likely to be met with resistance (Stevis, Morena, and Krause 2019). Indeed, many green stimulus measures adopted following the global financial crisis (GFC) were unpopular because they were seen to primarily benefit large corporate actors and/or wealthier members of society (IEA 2020e). As noted by the IEA (2020e), "the broader social and distributional impacts of any stimulus programme will receive increased scrutiny" in the COVID-19 context because the pandemic has disproportionately impacted low-income earners.

Many groups appealed to governments to make the COVID-19 recovery not only green but also just and equitable. For example, in Canada and the United States, hundreds of environmental, justice, labor, and movement organizations agreed to a set of principles for a just recovery (see www .justrecoveryforall.ca). International organizations, such as the OECD, also made special mention of "well-being and inclusiveness" in their recovery proposals (OECD 2020a).

Our conceptualization of a "green and just recovery" draws on climate/ energy justice and just transition literatures, which are explored in Section 2. While much of the just transition literature is focused on ensuring support for regions and communities economically dependent on fossil fuels as the world shifts to renewable energy, such a conceptualization is too narrow for our purposes. We do give particular attention to these communities, but in our view a green and just recovery must consider all populations that are vulnerable to the impacts of climate change and to the costs of the transition; existing inequities should be mitigated rather than reinforced. We therefore adopt the broader approach articulated by the Intergovernmental Panel on Climate Change (IPCC) that justice requires that "no people, workers, places, sectors, countries or regions are left behind in the move from a high carbon to a low-carbon economy" (IPCC 2022, 36).

1.3 Tracking the Recovery

The fact that there were numerous calls for a green and just recovery from the COVID-19 crisis from respected economists, academics, influential financial organizations, and civil society does not mean that this is what governments will deliver. As Gunn-Wright (2020, 70) points out, "Policymaking is not a science. It is a fight over whose problems get addressed, how those problems are addressed, and how public power and resources are distributed." In many countries around the world, key challenges related to complex energy reforms are political rather than technical. Stakeholders act to advance their own interests in power relationships associated with resource allocations. They support and block reforms accordingly. Lobbying for bailouts by fossil fuel firms and carbon-intensive industries such as aviation began almost as soon as the first COVID-19 lockdowns (see, e.g., Speers-Roesch 2020).

The GFC stimulus experience provides important lessons in this regard. The IEA (2020e) has noted that, overall, the recovery from the GFC was energy- and carbon-intensive. Tienhaara (2018) has demonstrated that in addition to the "dirty" stimulus funding, stakeholders, including large mining firms in Canada, the construction industry in Korea, and the fossil fuel industry in Australia and the United States, influenced the design and implementation of stimulus measures that were labeled "green."

Initial indications are that the COVID stimulus is not an improvement on the GFC stimulus and may in fact contribute even less to emissions reductions (O'Callaghan, Yau, and Hepburn 2022). The OECD (2020b) noted early on that governments were adopting a variety of concerning measures, including "plans to roll back existing environmental regulations ... reductions or waivers of environmentally-related taxes, fees and charges, unconditional bailouts of emissions-intensive industries or companies ... and increased subsidies to fossil-fuel intensive infrastructure ... and electricity consumers."

Several research groups and organizations have engaged in efforts to track the fiscal, monetary, and other policy measures that governments have developed in response to the COVID-19 pandemic. As these groups use different methodologies for determining what counts as a recovery measure, cover different countries, and define categories of green policies differently, they are difficult to compare (see Table 1). Nonetheless, the consensus appears to be that the outcome of recovery efforts to date has been disappointing and that the opportunity to "build back better" has been largely squandered. In October 2021, the groups behind four separate trackers signed a joint statement, noting that only 10–20 percent of stimulus could be classified as green and that "more effort is needed to secure a just and green recovery globally" (Energy Policy Tracker et al. 2021). The most recent study published (Nahm, Miller, and Urpelainen 2022) found that the G20 group of the twenty largest economies spent at least $14 trillion on recovery measures, but only 6 percent of that (about $860 billion) was allocated to areas that will also cut emissions, and almost 3 percent went to activities that are likely to increase global emissions. Indeed, the IEA estimated in July 2021 that the implementation of economic recovery measures would result in record-level CO_2 emissions in 2023 with "no clear peak in sight" (Frangoul 2021). On the other hand, it is worth noting that over time the amount of green stimulus has gradually increased (Welker, Roth, and Gerasimchuk 2022) and there were substantial commitments to green spending made in the United States in 2022 that fall outside of the coverage of several trackers and this study (see brief discussion in Section 4).

Table 1 Comparison of green stimulus trackers

Name of tracker/ weblink	Dates covered	Countries covered	Total stimulus analyzed (US$ trillion)	Green stimulus (US$ billion)	Proportion green
Energy Policy Tracker https://www .energypolicy tracker.org	2020 and 2021	G20+16+EU (+ 8 MDBs)	1.3 (energy-related only)	503	39% of energy related
OECD Green Recovery Database www.oecd.org/cor onavirus/en/ themes/green-recovery	Up to end of March 2022	OECD+6	3.3 (recovery spending)	1.1	33%
Vivid Economics www.vivideco nomics.com/case study/greenness-for-stimulus-index/	Up to end of June 2021	G20+10	17.2	1,800	10.5%

Table 1 (cont.)

Name of tracker/ weblink	Dates covered	Countries covered	Total stimulus analyzed (US$ trillion)	Green stimulus (US$ billion)	Proportion green
Global Recovery Observatory https://recovery .smithschool.ox .ac.uk/tracking/	Up to mid-December 2022	Fifty largest economies	18.2 (total spending) 3.1 (recovery spending)	970	5% of total spending, 31.2% of recovery
Green Recovery Tracker https://www .greenrecovery tracker.org/	2020 and 2021	EU (18)	0.86 (€0.72)	252 (€225)	29%
IEA Sustainable Recovery Tracker www.iea.org/ reports/sustain able-recovery- tracker	Up to end of March 2022	Fifty (IEA members +)	18.2	710	4%
Nahm et al. study	2020 & 2021	G20	14	860	6%

Notes on coverage: EPT = G20 + Bangladesh, Chile, Colombia, Egypt, Estonia, Finland, Kenya, the Netherlands, New Zealand, Nigeria, Philippines, Poland, Spain, Sweden, Ukraine, and Vietnam; Vivid = G20 + Colombia, Denmark, Finland, Iceland, Norway, Philippines, Singapore, Spain, Sweden, and Switzerland; OECD = OECD + Costa Rica (Accession), Brazil, China, India, Indonesia, and South Africa.

1.3.1 The Energy Policy Tracker

For this Element we utilize the EPT, developed by the International Institute for Sustainable Development (IISD) in partnership with the Institute for Global Environmental Strategies, Oil Change International, Overseas Development Institute, Stockholm Environment Institute, and Columbia University. The EPT covers investments and other relevant policies adopted in thirty-seven countries and the European Union as well as eight multilateral development banks (MDBs) (we focus on countries). The EPT showcases publicly available information on public money commitments for different energy types, and other policies supporting energy production and consumption in the following sectors: resources (e.g., extraction of oil, gas and coal, pipelines as well as restoration of extractive sites), power, buildings, mobility (e.g., airlines, airports, car manufacturing, rail and public transport, and cycling and walking), and other energy-intensive sectors.

The EPT was generated through a bottom-up approach, which involved collecting data on individual policies at an individual country level, and then aggregating them. The database was regularly updated between January 1, 2020, and December 31, 2021. Only new policies or amendments of existing policies were included in the EPT, and the majority of policies represent government responses to the COVID-19 pandemic. However, policies that had been designed before the crisis and introduced as planned after January 1, 2020, were also included. Even though these policies may not be directly linked to the COVID-19 pandemic, the fact that they were introduced despite sociopolitical disruptions and economic downturn is noteworthy. Both the date a policy is announced and when it is passed are registered in the EPT. The amount of funding committed to a policy is tracked, as well as the amount dispersed. However, given the data available at the time of our analysis, we only report funds committed.

Policies in the EPT are classified according to different criteria. One of the key criteria is a policy's environmental profile that depends on (1) which energy types it benefits, and (2) whether it has any environmental conditionality attached. Throughout the tracker, information is split across five categories: fossil unconditional, fossil conditional, clean unconditional, clean conditional, and other energy (see further Table 2).

1.4 Areas of Focus

For this research, we focus on policies in five areas that we identified as being the most significant for achieving decarbonization and reducing inequality: renewable energy, energy access, low-carbon mobility, energy-efficient

Table 2 Policy categories

Category	Description
Fossil unconditional	Policies that support production and consumption of fossil fuels (oil, gas, coal, "grey" hydrogen, or fossil fuel–based electricity) without any climate targets or additional pollution reduction requirements
Fossil conditional	Policies that support production or consumption of fossil fuels (oil, gas, coal, "blue" hydrogen, or fossil fuel–based electricity) with climate targets or additional pollution reduction requirements. The conditionality includes climate and pollution reduction targets as well as support to measures reducing environmental damage through carbon capture, utilization and storage, and end-of-the-pipe solutions such as reduction of methane leakages, extractive sites cleanup, and other measures
Clean unconditional	Policies that support production or consumption of energy that is both low-carbon and has negligible impacts on the environment if implemented with appropriate safeguards. These policies support energy efficiency and renewable energy coming from naturally replenished resources such as sunlight, wind, small hydropower, rain, tides, and geothermal heat. "Green" hydrogen, and active transport (cycling, walking) are also included
Clean conditional	Policies that are stated to support the transition away from fossil fuels, but unspecific about the implementation of appropriate environmental safeguards. Examples include large hydropower; rail public transport and electric vehicles (electric cars, bicycles, scooters, boats, etc.) using multiple energy types; smart grids and technologies to better integrate renewables; hydrogen in the case of mixed, but predominantly clean sources; and biofuels, biomass, and biogas with a proven minimum negative impact on the environment (sometimes referred to as "advanced," or "second," or "third generation"). Without appropriate

Table 2 (cont.)

Category	Description
	environmental safeguards, such policies can still have significant impacts. For instance, if powered with coal- or gas-based electricity, electric vehicle (EV) use is associated with significant emissions. Large hydropower has a negligible carbon footprint but can damage ecosystems. And even "advanced" biofuels can have a significant water footprint
Other energy	Policies outside of the two "fossil" and two "clean" buckets, or in both, fall in this umbrella category. These policies support nuclear energy (including uranium mining), "first-generation" biofuels, biomass and biogas (with proven negative impact on the environment), incineration, hydrogen of unspecified origin, and multiple energy types, for example, intertwined fossil fuels and clean energy (a sizable group, since many policies benefit both fossil and clean energy across the board)

Source: https://www.energypolicytracker.org/methodology/

buildings, and support for fossil fuel–dependent communities through worker retraining and environmental reclamation activities. Each of these categories is briefly explained below.

1.4.1 Renewable Energy

To facilitate an energy transition and achieve net-zero emissions by 2050, renewable energy technologies (e.g., solar, wind, hydro, tidal, and geothermal power) need to be developed and deployed on a large scale. In the IEA's Net-Zero by 2050 pathway, renewable energy generation needs to triple by 2030 and increase more than eightfold by 2050 (IEA 2021g). While this is a formidable challenge, the economics are favorable. Costs of renewable energy have fallen by an average of 18 percent annually since 2010 (Carbon Tracker Initiative 2021), undercutting the cheapest fossil fuels in many countries (IEA 2020h; IRENA 2021b). Although costs rose during the pandemic due to increased commodity prices and shipping costs, fossil fuel prices increased faster and thus the cost competitiveness of renewables still increased in this period (IEA 2022c). The International Renewable Energy Agency (IRENA 2021b) estimates that the 534 gigawatts of renewable energy capacity added since 2010 in emerging economies will reduce electricity generation costs up to $32 billion in 2021. Furthermore, the replacement of 800 gigawatts of coal-fired capacity would save $32 billion annually (IRENA 2021b). As electricity demand increases in emerging economies and new capacity is needed, renewable power generation projects will reduce costs by a minimum of $6 billion annually compared to the cost of adding the same capacity of fossil fuel–fired generation (IRENA 2021b). In addition to economic savings and GHG reductions, replacement of fossil fuels with renewable energy will reduce local air pollution, which in turn has positive impacts for human health and local environmental quality.

1.4.2 Energy Access

The IEA (2020g) defines energy access as "a household having reliable and affordable access to both clean cooking facilities and to electricity, which is considered enough to supply a basic bundle of energy services initially, and then increasing the level of electricity over time to reach the regional average." Universal energy access is necessary to fulfill both social and economic development, to satisfy needs for health, lighting, cooking, space, comfort, mobility, and communication (Edenhofer et al. 2011). In 2022, 775 million people lacked access to electricity, which was an increase of 20 million people compared with 2021, reversing the downward trend of the previous decade (Cozzi et al. 2022). Sub-Saharan Africa is the region with the lowest levels of energy access and greatest need for international support.

1.4.3 Low-Carbon Mobility

Redesigning the transport sector is considered vital to global climate change mitigation strategies (US EPA n.d.; IEA 2021f). Transport accounts for 37 percent of CO_2 emissions from end-use sectors and is more reliant on fossil fuels than any other sector (it is responsible for 57 percent of global oil demand) (IEA 2021e). Despite the stringency of COVID-19 lockdowns, which accounted for a 50 percent reduction of global road transport activity at the end of March 2020 and a 75 percent reduction in airline traffic in mid-April 2020 (IEA 2020d), mobility still accounted for 23 percent of energy-related CO_2 emissions at the end of March 2021 (IEA 2021f). The high emissions rate of carbon-intensive transportation in all its forms not only exacerbates climate change but also comes with well-documented risks to human health, as PM 2.5 pollution contributes to poor air quality, which in turn impacts morbidity and mortality rates (IPCC 2014; Mullen and Marsden 2016). Shifting transportation regimes away from a reliance on fossil fuels has benefits that extend beyond GHG emissions reductions. Improving public transit systems likewise improves road safety and increases employment, while also decreasing traffic congestion, urban sprawl, and various forms of noise and air pollution (Banister et al. 2011; Russo and Boutueil 2011; IPCC 2014).

1.4.4 Energy-Efficient Buildings

The construction and operation of buildings account for 35 percent of global energy use and 15 percent of CO_2 emissions (Global Alliance of Buildings and Construction 2021; IEA 2021d). Direct and indirect emissions from electricity and commercial heat used in buildings rose to 10 GtCO2 in 2019, the highest level ever recorded before dropping to 9Gt in 2020. The rise was driven by improved access to energy in developing countries, greater ownership and use of energy-consuming devices, and rapid growth in floor area. The drop in emissions in 2020 was primarily the result of less activity in the services sector during COVID-19 lockdowns and it is likely that emissions from this sector rebounded in 2021 (IEA 2021d). While space heating is currently responsible for around 45 percent of building-related emissions, energy demand for space cooling has more than tripled since 1990, making it the fastest-growing end use in buildings (Abergel and Delmastro 2020). The average temperature rise that comes with climate change is one of the factors contributing to increasing cooling service demand. There are clear links between building efficiency and inequality as low-income individuals and families are the most likely to live in inefficient homes, leading to higher heating and cooling costs as well as health impacts and reductions in quality of life.

1.4.5 Support for Fossil Fuel–Dependent Communities

While restructuring the energy sector to address climate change is likely to have a net-positive impact on employment, because more jobs will be created in sectors like renewable energy and energy efficiency than will be eliminated in sectors like fossil fuels, it is important to recognize that these shifts will create profound disruptions for affected workers and for communities and regions that are highly dependent on a single industry (UNFCCC Secretariat 2020). New green jobs may not appear at the same time or in the same location as old jobs are lost (UNFCCC Secretariat 2020). There are also understandable concerns from workers that they will be transitioning from unionized, high-paying jobs in the fossil fuel sector into nonunionized workplaces with lower wages and fewer benefits (Saha 2020). Policies in areas like worker retraining and income support are therefore needed to buffer the impacts of the energy transition and minimize human suffering (UNFCCC Secretariat 2020). In addition to lost employment opportunities, decades of resource extraction have left legacies for fossil fuel–dependent communities in terms of ongoing environmental and health impacts. Reclamation of these sites is critical from an environmental perspective as well as to meet health and equity objectives.

1.5 Methodology

For this research we had access to a more detailed database than that provided on the EPT website. This database included longer descriptions of policies and notes made by those inputting the data. This information was provided in English, with translation from other languages provided by those inputting the data.

We started by isolating policies that were coded in the EPT as "power generation," "mobility," and "buildings." We then calculated the overall amount of spending in those areas. Following this, we filtered the data in these categories to only include clean conditional and unconditional policies. In some cases, we also assessed how the funding was distributed to subcategories (e.g., different forms of renewable energy such as wind and solar). To assess whether governments had considered the potential distributive effects of the policies that fall into the clean categories, we developed a list of keywords based on our review of the literature (Section 2) and refined it following initial searches of the policy titles, descriptions, and notes in the database. The keywords were access, affordable/affordability, community(-ies), equity, equality, low income, marginalized, public, poor/poverty, and social. The policies that included these keywords were separated out of the dataset and then checked to ensure that the use of those words indicated that justice and/or equity was considered in policy design.

For energy access, we took a different approach as this was not a category that was pre-coded in the database. While we searched the entire database for references to energy access, we chose to primarily focus on policies in sub-Saharan African countries, given that these are the countries tracked in the EPT with the lowest levels of energy access. For support for fossil fuel–dependent communities, we searched the database for references to worker retraining and reclamation of orphaned/abandoned wells and mines. For this area, we did not exclude policies that fell under the "fossil conditional" or "fossil unconditional" categories.

Many policies did not pass an initial check. For example, a policy description might reference "affordability" but not contain any indication that it was targeted to a particular income bracket. Those policies that did pass were explored in greater depth through desk research, supplemented with twenty-five semi-structured interviews[1] (conducted via Zoom) with policy experts. We acknowledge that this method is imperfect, and we may have missed policies in the EPT that have a justice dimension but were not described using any of our keywords. However, we believe that we have captured the majority of relevant policies.

1.6 Limitations of the Research

Our research provides only a preliminary assessment of pandemic-era energy policies, for three key reasons. First, the pandemic had not ended at the time of writing. Although restrictions on economic activity had largely disappeared from much of the world, strict lockdowns were still in place in China and there is uncertainty about how future waves of the pandemic will impact economies and whether further stimulus spending will be required. Furthermore, additional crises, such as the 2022 energy crisis in Europe brought on by the Russian invasion of Ukraine, are adding further impetus for governments to invest in energy production and efficiency. Second, this Element is primarily the result of a desk study and does not provide in-depth case studies that could illuminate justice issues that we have missed or only scratch the surface of, particularly in the realm of procedural justice (i.e., who is and isn't involved in decision-making, what are the mechanisms for transparency and accountability in the allocation of funds, etc.). Third, many of the policies that we discuss have only recently been announced or rolled out and the implementation of these policies may diverge substantially from stated plans. Successful programs may be injected with further funding, while programs that run into difficulties may be streamlined or canceled entirely. Changes in government or in economic conditions may also result in programs being canceled prematurely. For example, research indicates that much of the GFC green stimulus proposed in 2009 was never actually delivered (Tienhaara 2018). Justice issues that are not apparent at the outset of policy plans may also arise during implementation. For all these reasons, this research should be considered exploratory. Further research, in the coming years, to follow up on the rollout and impacts of the COVID-19 recovery programs is merited.

Additionally, as we focus only on energy policies in five areas, we do not comprehensively address the question of whether the COVID-19 recovery has

---

[1] In the conduct of interviews, the authors followed an ethics protocol approved by the Queen's University General Research Ethics Board. Those interviewees who agreed to be named in the research are listed in the Appendix.

been green and just. There are many nonenergy sectors, such as agriculture, that also need to undergo a transition. Investments in protecting and expanding natural areas and biodiversity are also critical. Furthermore, a green and just recovery is not just about where money flows to but also where it is withheld from. Fossil fuel subsidies are a major economic barrier to reducing emissions as they encourage usage and allow the industry to "expand or build new . . . infrastructure that locks-in fossil fuel use" (Human Rights Watch 2021). Government subsidies to the sector artificially lowers the costs of fossil fuels and increases their economic viability while also sending the wrong signals to markets (Sanchez et al. 2021). Low-income, marginalized ethnic, and/or racial minority groups have experienced the greatest burden from fossil fuel extraction and have benefited the least from carbon-intensive energy production (White-Newsome, Meadows, and Kabel 2018; Crear-Perry and McAfee 2020). A key element of a green and just recovery that we do not address in this Element is for governments to cease public funding of fossil fuel production.

Finally, at a global level, a green and just recovery should involve substantial financial assistance flowing from the Global North to the Global South. The World Bank has emphasized that developing countries were experiencing a fourth wave of debt before the pandemic (Kose et al. 2021) and others have noted the long-lasting impacts of COVID-19 could delay an energy transition and the abilities of these countries to build back better (UNEP 2021). By late 2021, recovery spending per capita was almost 20 times higher in advanced economies than in emerging markets and developing economies and 200 times higher than in low-income economies (Energy Policy Tracker et al. 2021). While this aspect of the recovery is not the focus of this Element, we would emphasize that the pandemic only increases the urgency for the Global North to meet (and raise the level of) their commitments to international climate finance (Timperley 2021) and to also consider the case for climate reparations (Táíwò and Cibralic 2020).

2 Literature Review

Research on government investment in green sectors through green stimulus/ green economic recovery policy is generally located within the literature on green Keynesianism and green industrial policy, while justice and equity issues are addressed in separate literature on climate justice and just transitions. An emerging literature on "green new deals" attempts to merge some elements from both fields (see, e.g., Green and Healy 2022; Tienhaara and Robinson 2022). In this section, we review and integrate these bodies of literature with specific reference to the five key areas of energy policy that are the focus of our study.

2.1 Government Investment in Green Sectors

2.1.1 Green Keynesianism

According to Keynesian economics, during severe recession or depression, governments should inject money into the economy through public spending to increase demand for goods and services to achieve full employment. Although the COVID-19 recession differs substantially from previous ones, in that it was not induced by a conventional slump in demand or loss of confidence by the private sector, governments have overwhelmingly relied on fiscal measures to address it (O'Callaghan, Yau, and Hepburn 2022).

Green Keynesianism first emerged as a concept in Germany in the 1990s but was popularized in 2008 when governments around the world re-embraced Keynesian economics to address the GFC/Great Recession (Tienhaara 2018). Green Keynesians argue that governments should direct public spending in a manner that will contribute to environmental goals, such as GHG emissions reductions, in addition to economic ones. The extent to which the economic and environmental goals of green stimulus spending are either mutually reinforcing or at odds is the subject of ongoing debate.

As noted in Section 1.1, green sectors like renewable energy generation and building retrofitting are labor-intensive (Pollin et al. 2014; Garrett-Peltier 2017; Pollin and Chakraborty 2020). Although the labor intensity of projects in these sectors can change over time (e.g., the maintenance requirements for renewable energy installations are relatively minor), research indicates that they can still outperform projects in traditional energy sectors in terms of both direct and indirect job creation (O'Callaghan, Yau, and Hepburn 2022). While there are legitimate concerns about the quality and longevity of jobs created through government spending and the ability of displaced fossil fuel workers to enter into green sectors, these issues can be addressed through policy (see further Section 2.3.5).

A greater tension exists between the aim of boosting GDP and of addressing environmental issues. From an economic perspective, the performance of green stimulus measures in this regard has been mixed. The IEA (2020e) found that the overall macroeconomic effect of the GFC green stimulus programs was to boost GDP between 0.1 percent and 0.5 percent, which "could be counted as a success" given the severity of the crisis. However, growth impacts varied greatly by spending program. For example, GFC stimulus provided to renewable energy generation is regarded as having succeeded in reducing the cost of renewable energy technologies but having had little impact on GDP (Agrawala, Dussaux, and Monti 2020). From an environmental perspective, the goal of boosting GDP is inherently problematic due to a lack of evidence that economic growth can be decoupled from environmental harm quickly enough to avert the collapse of systems that support human civilization (Hickel and Kallis 2020). On the other hand, given that growth of certain economic sectors is necessary in the short term, government spending to induce economic recovery is not necessarily incompatible with a longer-term shift to a steady-state economy (Fiorino 2017; Pettifor 2019).

2.1.2 Green Industrial Policy

In the last decade, there has been renewed interest in policy circles in public investment in green sectors in the absence of an economic crisis and a subset of this known as "green industrial policy" (Meckling 2021). As Allan, Lewis, and Oatley (2021) note, this approach has even been embraced by conservative governments in countries like Britain.

Economist Dani Rodrik (2014) has been a key proponent of green industrial policy, arguing that public investment in green technologies is critical in the transition to a low-carbon economy. He suggests that green technologies are likely to be particularly prone to market failures because they are novel and involve a high level of investor risk. Furthermore, because the true social cost of carbon is not reflected in dirty forms of energy, the private return on investment in green technologies is significantly less than the social return. For these reasons, the private sector will not invest sufficiently in green technologies and so government subsidies and other forms of support are required, at least in the early stages of their development. Rodrick (2014) dismisses the traditional concern that governments are not good at "picking winners" and will consequently waste resources, suggesting that mistakes are inevitable (and are also made by market actors) and what is needed are mechanisms to recognize and correct mistakes. As for the concern that government intervention in the market invites rent-seeking behavior on the part of firms, this can also be overcome with appropriate policy design (Rodrik 2014).

There are a range of policies that governments can adopt under this approach, including providing financial assistance to the private sector through grants, below market loans, tax breaks, investments in research and development (R&D), local content requirements, and procurement policies (Allan et al. 2021). As Meckling et al. (2015) argue, green industrial policies can build up support for climate policy by increasing the number of actors that feel that they are benefiting from it.

Meckling (2021) argues that green industrial policy is primarily focused on increasing the competitiveness of a state in the global economy and contributing to economic growth. Given these goals, it is not clear that it will necessarily lead to the environmental outcomes, such as emissions reductions, that have been adopted as global objectives in treaties such as the Paris Agreement.

The notion of a "Green New Deal," which first emerged in the context of the GFC but was popularized in 2018 by US Congresswoman Alexandria Ocasio-Cortez and the Sunrise Movement, is often characterized as "a leftist resurrection of federal industrial policy" (Meyer 2019). However, Green New Deal proponents appear to be more influenced by climate justice and just transition discourses. They tend to take an intersectional approach and consider issues of race, gender, and economic equity as critical in policy design, something which is less evident in discussions of green industrial policy (Tienhaara and Robinson 2022). Allan et al. (2021) contend that a critical question for the future of green industrial policy is whether it will reduce inequality or, conversely, exacerbate it.

2.2 Climate Justice and a Just Transition

Discourses on climate justice and a just (energy) transition overlap substantially and are possibly merging in many contexts (Evans and Phelan 2016). For example, the definition provided in the most recent IPCC (2022) report that "no people, workers, places, sectors, countries or regions are left behind in the move from a high carbon to a low-carbon economy" goes beyond the traditional focus on workers in just transition discourses. However, given the distinct origins of these concepts, we first explore them separately in Sections 2.2.1–2.2.3.

2.2.1 Climate Justice

While there are many definitions of climate justice, they have all been influenced to some extent by the broader environmental justice literature and movement (Schlosberg and Collins 2014; Newell 2022). The earliest conceptualization of environmental justice was based on a recognition that marginalized communities are most likely to suffer the negative impacts of environmental damage (Schlosberg 2013). Such inequities arose from various forms of discrimination (e.g., based on race, gender, and/or class) (Galgóczi 2021). Climate justice applies these findings specifically to the issue of climate change, highlighting that the groups most vulnerable to the impacts of a warming planet (poor and marginalized communities in the Global South) are the least responsible for causing it, and conversely, those with prime responsibility (elites based in the Global North) are most insulated from harm (Kenner 2019).

While the North–South dimension is core to the concept of climate justice, increasingly scholars also consider inequality within countries and not only the

uneven causes/impacts of climate change but also the distributional effects of
the policies intended to address it. As Galgóczi (2021, 542) argues:

> Even within societies, different income groups have different responsibilities
> for causing climate change and are exposed to its effects in an asymmetrical
> manner. Lower income households tend to have occupations that are more
> exposed to climate change, for example in sectors such as agriculture,
> construction, tourism and health care. The housing conditions of the poor
> make them also more vulnerable (e.g., inner city "heat islands" vs. green
> belts).... When the costs and burdens attached to necessary climate policies
> affect lower income groups more, this may even turn into a "triple injustice."

A strand of literature specifically focused on energy policy and energy systems
has emerged in the last decade (McCauley et al. 2013). Energy justice scholars
consider, for example, the distributional injustices that might arise through the
siting of energy infrastructure as well as limited access to energy services
(Jenkins et al. 2016).

In addition to questions of distributional justice, climate justice and energy
justice scholars also consider procedural justice; that is, who is able to participate in decision-making and whether climate policies provide for inclusivity,
transparency, and accountability (Jenkins et al. 2016; Initiative for Energy
Justice 2019; Siciliano et al. 2021). Related to this is recognition justice,
which is about who is considered a valid participant in climate policy decision-
making procedures (Newell 2022).

2.2.2 Just Transition

The concept of a just transition came out of the North American labor movement in the 1970s and is now widely embraced by unions as well as the
International Labour Organization (ILO) (Stevis and Felli 2015). Arguably, it
emerged in response to the decline of the social welfare state in the United
States and Canada (Stevis 2023). While originally centered within unions in the
chemicals sector, the just transition is now most associated with fossil fuel
industry workers and communities reliant on that industry. At the core of the just
transition is the notion of fair burden-sharing (Galgóczi 2021). In countries
where carbon-intensive sectors like fossil fuel extraction are concentrated in
specific regions (e.g., the province of Alberta in Canada), a just transition entails
job retraining for those active in the sector but also programs to support all those
whose livelihood is connected to the industry. In addition to such arrangements,
the idea of a just transition also encapsulates the notion that affected workers
and communities will be meaningfully engaged in decision-making processes
(Santos Ayllón and Jenkins 2023).

2.2.3 Our Approach

In our assessment of policies adopted by governments during the pandemic, distributional justice is our primary focus. We aim to assess whether, in addition to aiming to reduce GHGs, governments also aimed to increase the availability and affordability of energy (including through energy-efficient technologies and low-carbon mobilities) for low-income, marginalized and vulnerable communities and/or to create decent jobs for low-skilled workers or workers at risk of unemployment or underemployment in the energy transition. We recognize that procedural justice and recognition justice are also critical. However, given that energy policies adopted during the pandemic are still in the very early stages of development, and the fact that this is primarily a desk-based study, these issues cannot be explored in any depth.

2.3 Public Investment Needs and Justice Dimensions in Specific Focus Areas

2.3.1 Renewable Energy

The pandemic initially had a negative impact on deployment of renewable energy. In the first half of 2020, global renewable electricity capacity additions were more than 11 percent lower than in the first six months of 2019. However, renewable energy developers accelerated installations when restrictions on economic activities were lifted to make up for delays (IEA 2020a). In 2021, a record-breaking 6 percent addition in renewable capacity occurred despite ongoing supply-chain challenges and continued construction delays associated with the pandemic (IEA 2022c).

Although the progress in increasing renewable energy capacity during the pandemic is welcome, much greater investment in the sector is needed. IRENA estimates that investments of $2 trillion toward renewables and other transition-related technologies are needed between 2021 and 2023 and should grow to $4.5 trillion by 2030. This level of investment would increase renewable power generation five times faster than it has in recent years, allowing for a more rapid phaseout of fossil fuels (IRENA 2020).

Governments invest in renewable energy through a wide variety of policy mechanisms. Fiscal incentives such as feed-in-tariffs, which provide a fixed price to renewable energy providers over a period of time, are particulary popular and have been shown to be effective (Lewis 2021). Governments also provide support for R&D in renewable energy generation and storage. Additionally, upgrades and modifications of infrastructure to support renewable energy, particularly electricity grids, are critical and often the responsibility of governments (Seetharaman et al. 2019; IEA 2020f).

Investments in renewable energy have the potential to improve energy access, reduce energy poverty, and create employment opportunities (Dincer 2000; Edenhofer et al. 2011). These outcomes are more likely when they are targeted to marginalized and underserved communities, particularly remote communities (i.e., not connected to the main electricity grid) that are currently dependent on fossil fuels for energy. Several policies identified in our screening of the EPT fall into this category and are highlighted in Section 3.1. Policies promoting or funding renewable energy projects that are community-led or community-owned are also examined. We acknowledge that there has been a tendency "to assume rather than demonstrate that community projects are more democratic or just" (Van Veelen 2018, 645). Therefore, we stress that this is a preliminary review and more in-depth case studies would be required to assess whether, for example, there were certain societal groups that were excluded or marginalized in the initiatives that we highlight (van Bommel and Höffken 2021).

2.3.2 Energy Access

The COVID-19 pandemic has made the goal of providing universal energy access by 2030 significantly more difficult to achieve. The financial impact of the pandemic has reversed progress on energy access in countries like Nigeria, the Democratic Republic of Congo, and Ethiopia (IRENA 2021a). It is estimated that the pandemic could increase levels of extreme poverty for an additional 70 million rural people throughout both South Asia and sub-Saharan Africa (Laborde Debucquet, Martin, and Vos 2020). Due to the containment measures for the COVID-19 virus, many of those who worked in informal jobs became unemployed and experienced difficulty paying for energy services (Zaman, van Vliet, and Posch 2021). Approximately 30 million people who previously could afford access to energy are now unable to (IRENA 2021a).

The post-COVID-19 global economic environment will include a long-term recession, as well as increased levels of unemployment as countries work toward restarting their economies (SEforALL 2020), which will contribute further to a decline in energy access. If the impacts of the COVID-19 pandemic on achieving energy access go ignored, the Sustainable Development Goal (SDG) of universal access to affordable, sustainable energy by 2030 (SDG 7) will not be achieved.

Investment into renewable energy generation will have to be around $550–850 billion per year, alongside other investments into electricity networks, to reach universal energy access by 2030, which is significantly higher than the current annual \$300 billion investment (IRENA 2021a). In Africa alone, to achieve universal electricity access by 2030, an annual investment of around \$29–30 billion in electricity infrastructure is required (SEforALL 2020; Cozzi et al. 2022). Least developed countries face the greatest challenges in accessing finance for energy projects (Bhattacharyya 2013).

Energy infrastructure plans must be socially and culturally inappropriate, taking into consideration community values, especially in rural areas (Tarekegne 2020). Renewable energy can create more added value when generated locally, especially for rural locations that are not connected to the national grid (Khennas 2012). Off-grid solutions (see Table 3) should actively be considered for deployment in areas that have lower consumption levels, as they have the potential to provide greater improvements to energy access per dollar spent (Bhattacharyya and Palit 2016). However, the pandemic hit the off-grid sector hard; about two-thirds of mini-grid operators and 75 percent of solar home system suppliers were facing critical liquidity challenges during the first phase of the COVID-19 crisis (IEA 2020g).

To enhance the deployment of off-grid energy systems, countries will need to engage in land-use reforms and streamlining of regulatory processes that act as barriers to the deployment of electricity systems (Mugisha et al. 2021). Research indicates that a community-ownership model increases the likelihood of off-grid projects succeeding (Duran and Sahinyazan 2021).

Only two countries tracked in the EPT – Kenya and Nigeria – lack universal access to electricity and rolled out programs to address this during 2020–1. We describe these programs in Section 3.2.

2.3.3 Low-Carbon Mobility

The pandemic and associated lockdowns necessitated that human mobility be reduced to curb the spread of COVID-19. While this reduced the use of personal vehicles and associated GHG emissions, it also dramatically impacted the use of public transportation such as buses and trains. Public transportation systems remained underutilized even as lockdowns eased, as they were considered a vector of virus transmission (Gutiérrez, Miravet, and Domènech 2021). As revenue from fare collection plummeted, government support was needed simply to maintain basic transportation services and to keep workers employed (Vickerman 2021). The loss of revenue may, in some cases, result in reduced service into the future and delays in investments in areas such as fleet electrification.

Table 3 Types of electricity systems and their advantages and disadvantages

Type of system	Description	Advantages	Disadvantages	Energy source
Main grid	A main grid consists of complicated interconnections, including three main sections: generation, transmission, and distribution. Electricity is transmitted through power lines. With a distribution grid, substations are connected for customers that require electricity	• Reduced energy losses • Efficient electrical generation • Reduced operations and management costs for utilities • Lower power costs for consumers	• Costly to expand grid • Expansion through various political jurisdictions • Requires political power that disadvantaged populations lack • Requires supporting networks to move forward generation • Not viable for most rural areas	• Coal • Natural gas • Wind • Solar power • Hydro
Off-grid: mini-grid	Mini-grids consist of small-scale electricity generation (10 kW to 10 MW) that serves limited consumers through a grid that is separate from the national transmission network. The systems can offer energy that ranges from covering a small	• Offers a collective solution • Lower in cost • Productive source of electricity • Assists in economic development • Can be connected to main power grid eventually • More energy security	• High initial cost • Higher system failure rates due to poor maintenance	• Wind • Small hydro • Solar power • Diesel

	number of households and commercial consumers or entire villages	• Less environmentally degrading • Can overcome energy isolation barriers • Can be run by the public utility, private sector, community-based, or a combination of models		
Off-grid: solar household system (SHS)	PV systems are an option for rural areas that are isolated from the grid. It can extend a fixed amount of electricity per day. It is often placed on top of a rooftop to capture sunlight, a battery for storing energy, and end-use appliances with a capacity between 10 W and 200 W	• Indirect benefits related to social, economic, and environmental factors • After initial cost the investment cost is reduced overtime • Increase in quality of life due to access to light	• High connection cost • Fixed amount of energy • Higher system failure rates due to poor maintenance	• PV solar power

Source: Authors (based on Mahapatra and Dasappa 2012; Alstone, Gershenson, and Kammen 2015; Hansen, Pedersen, and Nygaard 2015; Williams et al. 2015; Adeleke 2016; Baurzhan and Jenkins 2016; Bhattacharyya and Palit 2016; Kagimu and Ustun 2016; Nkiriki and Ustun 2017; Akinyele, Belikov, and Levron 2018; IRENA 2021b)

The C40 network of cities has argued that "public transport can play a major role in supporting a green and just economic recovery," highlighting that public transport networks "enable affordable access to the economic, social and cultural opportunities offered by cities especially for those who cannot afford to own a vehicle" (C40, International Transport Workers' Federation 2021). Public support for active transportation can also contribute to equity if programs recognize and work to remove barriers that prevent certain groups from participating in cycling and walking (McCullough, Lugo, and Stokkum 2019; Agyeman 2020). Electrically assisted micromobility modes (e.g., e-scooters, e-bikes) can also increase access to active transport, increase the distance that people are willing to commute using active transportation, and help with difficult topographies (Koehl 2021).

Municipalities have significant involvement in enabling and encouraging public and active modes of transport. The notion of the "eco-city" gained popularity in the wake of the pandemic as a means for municipalities to take a holistic approach to transitioning mobility systems. Broadly, the goal of an eco-city is to:

> [provide] healthy abundance to its inhabitants without consuming more (renewable) resources than it produces, without producing more waste than it can assimilate, and without being toxic to itself or neighboring ecosystems. Its inhabitants' ecological impact reflect planetary supportive lifestyles; its social order reflects fundamental principles of fairness, justice and reasonable equity. (Ecocity Builders and International Ecocity Framework & Standards 2010)

Generally, eco-cities center around low-carbon discourses, "green-smart" technological innovation, and accessibility to transport for all peoples (Joss, Cowley, and Tomozeiu 2013; van Dijk 2015). However, it should be noted that the concept of the eco-city has also been subject to thorough critique, with some scholars questioning whether the concept provides more than a "technological fix" (Joss, Cowley, and Tomozeiu 2013; Caprotti 2014). One eco-city program is captured in the EPT and is discussed in Section 3.3.

In addition to public and active modes of transportation, a switch from internal combustion engine vehicles to EVs is widely considered to be an essential part of the transition to low-carbon mobility. While there is now a technology and cost breakthrough for EV and battery production, these technologies are still largely confined to wealthier markets (Henderson 2020; Dolšak and Prakash 2022).

Consumer subsidies have been a popular method to increase the uptake of EVs (O'Callaghan and Murdock 2021). During 2020, EV registrations increased by 41 percent, despite the overall 16 percent drop in global car sales, with approximately 3 million electric cars sold globally in 2020 (IEA 2021b). In 2021, sales of EVs doubled from the previous year to a new record of 6.6 million (IEA 2022b), which was again surpassed in 2022 with 10 million units sold (IEA 2023). The IEA attributes this resilience to an increased number of consumer subsidies that governments used to continue to incentivize EV sales during the pandemic, citing a global increase of $14 billion in government spending for electric car sales in 2020 and more than double that in 2021 (IEA 2021b, 2022b).

It is important to recognize that EV subsidies primarily benefit high-income earners (Ku and Graham 2022) although there have been efforts in some jurisdictions to target subsidies to low-income earners (California's program is discussed in Section 3.3) (Linn 2022). Targeted subsidies make economic sense because a rebate or grant is more likely to influence a low-income earner's decision to purchase an EV (wealthier households are more likely to be "free riders" who would have purchased an EV in the absence of a subsidy) (DeShazo and Di Filippo 2021). Low-income earners also tend to drive older, less-efficient cars; getting these cars off the road will have a greater impact on emissions while also promoting upward mobility for low-income households that will save on fuel costs and vehicle repairs (Bauer, Hsu, and Lutsey 2021; Aoun 2022). In addition to targeted subsidies, making purchases of used EVs eligible for rebates can also significantly increase the number of potential beneficiaries of a program (DeShazo and Di Filippo 2021).

Increased investment is also needed for improving and expanding charging infrastructure to ensure not only that are there available electric chargers for an increased number of EVs, but also that the electric grid itself is decarbonized (IEA 2021g). However, equity issues can arise if infrastructure is unevenly distributed, leading to "urban charging deserts" in some neighborhoods (often those where racial minorities are dominant) or if gentrification occurs in areas where charging stations are concentrated (Henderson 2020; Liang et al. 2023). The private sector also lacks incentives to invest in charging infrastructure in remote areas, and active public sector involvement is needed to ensure that these areas are not neglected (Moerenhout 2021).

While there is no doubt that electric mobility will play a key role in the energy transition, there are several environmental and justice concerns associated with *mass uptake* of personal EVs. Scholars have noted that promotion of mass uptake of EVs locks in car-focused urban design and limits space available for public and active modes of transportation (Henderson 2020). There are also concerns associated with the resource extraction that is required for EV

Table 4 Types of building energy efficiency retrofits

	Minor	**Major**	**Deep energy**
Financial cost	Low	Low to medium	High
Upgrade examples	Lighting	Heating/cooling	Entire structure
Energy use reduction	≤10%	10–30%	≥50%
Impact	Low	Medium	High

Source: Sustainable Buildings Canada 2021

batteries, which could be limited through efforts to increase use of public transportation and limit car dependency (Hund et al. 2020; Riofrancos et al. 2023).

2.3.4 Energy-Efficient Buildings

In late 2020, the Global Alliance of Buildings and Construction (2020) called the global COVID-19 pandemic an opportunity for a "paradigm shift" in the buildings sector through recovery package measures to promote building decarbonization. This is not the first crisis to have been viewed as an opportunity to improve the energy efficiency of buildings. When proposals for green stimulus measures were circulated in 2008 and 2009 in the wake of the GFC, there appeared to be one point of agreement between proposal authors: increasing the energy efficiency of buildings was a "low-hanging fruit" that was ripe and ready to be picked (Green New Deal Group 2008; UNEP 2009). The fact that this fruit remained available for picking in 2020 indicates that the opportunity presented by the GFC was not seized; although there certainly were some investments in building efficiency made by governments, they were small compared to what was needed (Tienhaara 2018).

Renovating existing buildings can be a relatively cheap way to create significant energy savings and emission reductions. Examples of energy efficiency measures in buildings include sealing gaps, installing insulation, and upgrading windows with double- or triple-glazed panes. Investments in these areas can "offer an ongoing stream of cost savings that [are] generally far greater than the value of the initial investment" (Brownlee 2013; Hoicka, Parker, and Andrey 2014). Minor or one-off retrofits are cost-effective and practical options in many contexts (see Table 4). However, the most substantial GHG reductions occur through deep energy retrofits. Deep energy retrofits are high cost, high impact changes of the entire building structure (Sustainable Buildings Canada 2021). This class of building retrofits reduces the structure's energy use by 30–50 percent (IEA 2020b). Additionally, retrofits can prepare buildings to support increased renewable energy, resilient microgrids, and EVs. Retrofits are also beneficial because keeping older buildings for longer means avoiding the substantial emissions associated with construction.

There are several barriers to the voluntary adoption of energy efficiency measures in buildings. Private actors have tended to view investments in energy-efficient buildings as risky and inconvenient (Baldoni et al. 2019). The retrofitting of existing buildings requires a high upfront cost for investors, which pays off in the long run rather than short term, through benefits like reduced overall energy expenditure (Baldoni et al. 2019). There are also information barriers; many building owners are simply unaware of potential cost savings associated with energy efficiency measures (Calder 2020). Additionally, for many owners there is uncertainty about whether they will own or live in a building long enough to collect a return on the investment (Brownlee 2013). In the rental market, there is a conflict of interest between the owner who would have to make the investment and the occupier who would often reap the rewards through lower energy costs (Economidou 2018). Finally, fluctuations in the cost of electricity and fossil fuels can affect the cost–benefit analysis of building upgrades (Persram 2011). These barriers can be reduced with public investments, for example through grants and loans.

If designed well, building energy efficiency policies can reduce both GHG emissions and energy poverty, which is closely connected to health and social inequality (Boemi and Papadopoulos 2019). Energy poverty can lead to respiratory and cardiovascular problems, and preventable deaths in winter or during periods of extreme heat. High heating and cooling expenditures disproportionately impact populations at the lower end of the socioeconomic spectrum. Braubach and Ferrand (2013, 331) make the case that lower-income households are "three times more vulnerable to indoor cold than the other households." Low-income residences are also the least likely to be upgraded in the absence of government support (Kantamneni and Haley 2022). This is because low-income households lack the necessary upfront capital to invest in retrofits. Additionally, a focus on low-income households in government programs is likely to reduce free rider effects (public funds going to households that would have made investments anyway) and rebound effects (recipients of energy efficiency improvements increase energy use and offset the savings) (Lee, Kung, and Owen 2011).

In addition to reducing energy poverty and emissions, investing in energy-efficient buildings has significant potential for skilled job creation, particularly given the low barriers to entry into the retrofit industry (UNFCCC Secretariat 2020). According to Wei, Patadia, and Kammen (2010), energy efficiency investment "offers a high payoff in induced jobs." Garrett-Peltier (2017) estimates that for every $1 million invested, 7.72 full-time equivalent (FTE) jobs in energy efficiency are created, versus 2.65 FTE jobs in the fossil fuel industry. Importantly, building energy efficiency jobs are not limited geographically and can therefore provide much needed employment opportunities in rural areas and small towns (Haley 2020). A just transition also requires that attention be paid to ensuring that these jobs have good work conditions and pay well.

2.3.5 Support for Fossil Fuel–Dependent Communities

Although the COVID-19 economic crisis differs from previous crises in important ways (Cohan 2020; International Labour Organization 2020), it has, nevertheless, led to increased unemployment, which has in turn exacerbated economic and social inequality (International Labour Organization 2021). A total of 255-million FTE jobs (assuming a 48-hour working week) or 8.8 percent of global working hours were lost in 2020 relative to the fourth quarter of 2019 (International Labour Organization 2021). Working hours rebounded in 2021, but deteriorated again in early 2022, even though most workplace closures had, by that time, ended (International Labour Organization 2022).

As noted in Section 1, many carbon-intensive sectors were hit hard by the pandemic. The price of oil collapsed in 2020 and so too did employment in the sector. In the United States, about 107,000 oil and gas workers were laid off between March and August 2020 (Dickson et al. 2020). However, even prior to 2019, workers in the sector were vulnerable to fluctuations in the oil price and to increased automation (Saha 2020). In the long term, the increasing cost competitiveness of renewable energy coupled with government-imposed limits on extraction should lead to a contraction of the fossil fuel industry and associated loss of jobs in the sector.

Providing (re)training support to workers, in the form of subsidized or free education and relevant work experience, is key to a green and just recovery, even if it alone will not address all issues related to employment disruptions. Although much of the emphasis is put on retraining/upskilling fossil fuel workers to work in emerging green sectors, a just transition should also consider other workers who are indirectly impacted by a loss of economic activity in an area when an industry shuts down (Gass 2021).

Experts argue that worker retraining cannot be left in the hands of corporations. As Ana Guerra, National Chapter Director of Iron & Earth (a not-for-profit worker-led organization in Canada) notes, "There has to be some sort of regulatory system in place ... because otherwise ... How far can a corporation go? It will go towards what their shareholders say" (interview with Ana Guerra, 2021). There are government and nonprofit organizations that were operating prior to the COVID-19 pandemic that focus on helping workers transition into jobs in the renewable energy sector. For example, Skills Development Scotland (Scotland's national job agency since 2008) was able to retrain and upskill more than 3,000 fossil fuel employees from 2016 to 2019 in partnership with Scotland's energy task force. Iron & Earth has been involved in oil and gas worker retraining in Canada since 2015. However, greater investment on the part of many governments is needed. David Coyne from Skills Development Scotland argues the government simply "hasn't fully understood the scale of investment that's going to be required to help people reskill and upskill and nor have they fully understood the pace at which we may need to move" (interview with David Coyne, 2021). Iron & Earth estimates that retraining a single worker can cost about CAD10,000 ($7957) (interview with Ana Guerra, 2021).

In addition to greater investment in retraining, it is also critical that programs and policies reflect the gendered dimensions of the transition (International Labour Organization 2015; UNFCCC Secretariat 2020; Just Transition Initiative 2021), particularly considering the severe impacts that the pandemic has had on women. Attention should also be given to issues such as worker safety, fair wages, and respect for workers' rights (International Labour Organization 2015; UNFCCC Secretariat 2020; Just Transition Initiative 2021). In developing worker (re)training policies, governments should provide opportunities for meaningful participation from impacted workers communities (Stanford 2021) and representation from Indigenous peoples (interview with Ana Guerra, 2021). Ultimately, policies and programs will vary by country as they will have to be designed to address the specific needs of workers in very different contexts (International Labour Organization 2015; UNFCCC Secretariat 2020).

Reclamation of mines and oil and gas wells is also a critical justice issue for fossil fuel–dependent communities. In addition to the environmental and health benefits associated with cleaning up oil and gas wells and coal mines, such activities can also create employment opportunities (Raimi, Nerurkar, and Bordoff 2020; Boettner 2021). If locals, including former oil and gas workers and miners, are given priority access to these jobs, it contributes further to the achievement of a just transition (French 2020). Moreover, site restoration can make land available for new community amenities and developments, including renewable energy projects.

Idle and abandoned/orphaned oil and gas wells can leak gas, oil, saline water, and other fluids (Kang et al. 2021), which in turn can "contribute to local adverse environmental and human health effects from soil and groundwater contamination" (Alboiu and Walker 2019, 1). Abandoned wells also leak large amounts of methane – a potent GHG – into the atmosphere (Boettner 2021). Methane leaks also risk explosions occurring (Boettner 2021; Kang et al. 2021). Plugging wells can eliminate some of these risks, but full restoration would also involve site decontamination and revegetation (Boettner 2021). Oil and gas wells are located in both residential (often low-income and racially marginalized communities, see Mernit 2021) and rural areas. Inactive, aging wells have been a large burden for farmers, who often do not have the option to refuse wells on their property (CBC Radio 2020).

Abandoned coal mines also present serious harm to human health and the environment. Many abandoned coal mines emit acid mine drainage that can have "long-term devastating impacts on groundwater, community water supplies, rivers, streams, and aquatic life" (GroundWater Protection Council n.d.).

The pandemic and downturn in the oil, gas, and coal industries has potentially made it harder to ensure that reclamation is paid for by companies. For example, across Canada and the United States there were at least 116,245 oil and gas wells that were operated by companies that were filing for bankruptcy in the first half of 2020 (Kang et al. 2021). This suggests a role for governments in the form of targeted recovery policies.

2.4 Summary

Substantial government investment in renewable energy generation and distribution (including increased access to energy in some countries), technologies and infrastructure for low-carbon mobility, and energy efficiency of buildings is necessary to decarbonize economies and avert climate breakdown. Governments have an opportunity to further the goals of climate justice and a just transition at the same time as they reduce GHGs if they consider the distributional impacts of energy policies and target them to low-income, marginalized and underserved communities. Furthermore, ensuring specific support for communities that are dependent on the fossil fuel industry for employment will help to ensure that the transition does not create new inequities and injustices. Targeted policies will be somewhat context dependent (e.g., there are more underserved remote communities in large, sparsely populated countries like Australia and Canada) but across policy areas, it is evident that providing low-income earners with greater support is likely to contribute to program efficacy as well as contributing to equity objectives.

3 Energy Policies during the Pandemic

For the period 2020–1, governments and MDBs tracked in the EPT developed new or amended energy policy measures providing $1.3 trillion in support, at least 40 percent ($519.38 billion) of which was for fossil fuels ($389.23 billion unconditional, $130.15 billion conditional), 39 percent ($503.4 billion) for clean energy ($132.67 billion unconditional, $370.77 billion conditional), and 21 percent ($276.48 billion) for other energy (see Figure 1). Over 94 percent of this spending was from governments, with the remainder coming from the MDBs. The distribution of funds by the top ten spending leaders (representing over 70 percent of all spending captured in the EPT) is provided in Figure 2. We do not attempt to quantify the number of policies that have equity/justice elements. However, another study based on the EPT (using a different methodology) has estimated that 11 percent of energy policies approved between January 2020 and November 2021 are likely to decrease inequality (Dufour, Roth, and Picciariello 2022).

3.1 Renewable Energy

The EPT contained information on power generation policies by governments amounting to $255 billion. Of this, $34.7 billion was allocated to clean conditional policies and $34.1 billion was for clean unconditional policies. A further $20.6 billion went to fossil conditional policies and $13.8 billion to fossil unconditional policies (see Figure 3). Most funds ($151.7 billion) were in the "other energy" category, which includes policies that cover multiple sources of

■ Clean conditional   ■ Clean unconditional ■ Fossil conditional
■ Fossil unconditional ■ Other energy

Figure 1 Public spending by category, Jan. 2020–Dec. 2021
(**Source:** Authors, based on EPT 2022)

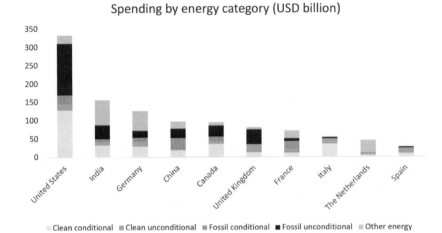

Figure 2 Public spending in top ten countries, Jan. 2020–Dec. 2021
(**Source:** Authors, based on EPT 2022)

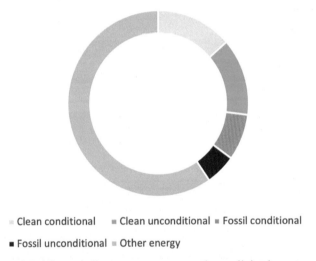

Figure 3 Public spending on power generation policies by category,
Jan. 2020–Dec. 2021
(**Source:** Authors, based on EPT 2022)

energy ($120 billion) (e.g., infrastructure for electrical transmission and storage, $33.5 billion) and nuclear energy ($11.8 billion).

Projects involving multiple energy types or multiple renewables received most of the clean funding, followed by hydroelectric projects and hydrogen projects (see Figure 4). The largest investments were from the United States, with a $10 billion increase to the borrowing authority of the Bonneville Power Authority to

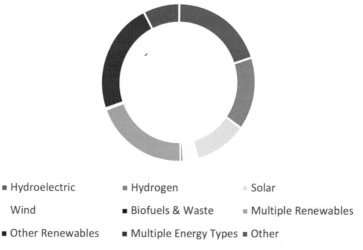

- Hydroelectric   - Hydrogen   Solar

  Wind   - Biofuels & Waste   - Multiple Renewables

- Other Renewables   - Multiple Energy Types - Other

Figure 4 Public spending on clean conditional and clean unconditional power generation policies by type of energy, Jan. 2020–Dec. 2021

Source: Authors, based on EPT 2022

aid in the reconstruction and replacement of the Federal Columbia River Power System, and $3 billion allocated to the Smart Grid Investment Matching Grant Program, a program initially funded under the Obama administration's GFC stimulus (Evans 2022). Germany made a $9.1 billion investment in hydrogen. Twelve EU member states made a collective investment of €2.9 billion ($3.3 billion) in the European Battery Innovation project (European Commission 2021). This project will support research and innovation along the entire battery value chain, starting from extraction of materials to recycling and disposal. Public funding is expected to encourage an additional €9 billion ($10.5 billion) from private investments. The project is expected to be completed by 2028 (European Commission 2021).

Other policies with a large monetary commitment have been implemented by Italy. The national government has committed nearly €5.2 billion ($5.5 billion) for three separate policies related to power generation (Government of Italy 2021). The first €2.4 billion ($2.5 billion) policy focuses on electricity generation and supporting economies in small municipalities at risk of depopulation. The investment will install 2,000 MW of new electricity generation and produce 2,500 GWh per year to reduce GHG emissions by about 1.5 million tons of CO_2 per year. The second €1.6 billion ($1.7 billion) policy focuses on incentivizing the installation of solar energy panels on buildings to improve the agricultural sector while simultaneously redeveloping structures in need of asbestos removal and improvements to insulation and ventilation. Finally, the third

€1.2 billion ($1.3 billion) policy aims to install production capacity from agrovoltaic plants and produce 1,000 GWh per year to reduce about 0.8 million tons of CO_2. The policy focuses on making a more competitive agricultural sector and providing a hybrid agriculture-energy production system without damaging the land.

While the national government in Australia focused on a "gas-led recovery" (Morton 2020) and made only small investments in renewables (see Section 3.1.1), both Queensland and Victoria had large funding programs. The Queensland state government committed AUD2 billion ($1.03 billion) toward the establishment of a Queensland renewable energy and hydrogen jobs fund. This investment will allow "energy government-owned corporations to increase ownership of commercial renewable energy and hydrogen projects, as well as supporting infrastructure, including in partnership with the private sector" (Queensland Treasury 2021). The fund will consider investment proposals from government-owned corporations that support renewable energy generation and storage to aid in meeting Queensland's 50 percent renewable energy target by 2030. Such proposals can include "solar, wind, pumped hydroelectric storage, hydrogen and supporting network infrastructure" (Queensland Treasury 2021). Victoria's program is particularly notable for the efforts being made by the government to increase community consultation – we briefly summarize it in Box 1 given the relevance to procedural justice, which as noted in Section 2 is a key aspect of climate justice but not one that we focus on in this Element.

Governments in India also introduced several policies to increase renewable energy power generation. The government of Maharashtra, for example, announced a clean unconditional policy that aims to implement 17,360 MW of transmission system-connected renewable power projects by 2025. This is divided into 12,930 MW of solar power projects, 2,500 MW of wind energy projects, and 1,350 MW of cogeneration projects. It will also include 100,000 agricultural solar pumps, 52,000 kV of rooftop solar systems, 2,000 solar water supply stations, the electrification of 10,000 rural homes, microgrid projects for twenty homes, 55,000 square feet of solar water and cooking systems, and 800 solar cold storage projects (Maharashtra Energy Development Agency 2021). The state government of Andhra Pradesh also launched a project to generate 10,000 MW of solar power. The government has promised nine hours of free power each day to the agricultural sector for the next thirty years. This sector currently consumes approximately 24 percent of total energy demand in the state (TNN Agency 2020). Finally, Korea also invested in renewables as part of its ₩73.4 trillion ($57 billion) Green New Deal (Chowdhury 2021; IEA 2021h).

Box 1 Victoria, Australia

On February 18, 2021, the Victorian Government announced a AUD1.2 billion ($850 million) clean energy package as part of the state budget to invest in renewables, grid infrastructure, energy efficiency, and decarbonization projects. Within this budget is a proposed AUD540 million ($380 million) to be used over the four years toward the establishment of six renewable energy zones (REZs) to bring 600 megawatts of renewable energy generation online. This investment would allow Victoria to transition from a system of a few large electricity generators to a system that connects many renewable projects across the REZs. An REZ is a renewable-rich area with infrastructure and a transmission network that can supply clean energy to other areas that need it, ensuring a secure, affordable, clean, and reliable energy system and storage. Renewable energy zones will be located in Central North, Gippsland, Murray River, Ovens Murray, South Victoria, and Western Victoria and will help direct investments to enhance transmissions grids. The Department of Environment, Land, Water and Planning in the Victorian Government has specifically stated that these REZs will "ensure that communities, including traditional owners, are engaged in the process." Along with the implementation of REZs, a portion of funding will be put toward the establishment of a new body, VicGrid, to oversee investments in the grid. This body will work closely with local communities and traditional owners to ensure that all stakeholders receive benefits from REZs. By ensuring community consultation at the beginning of the planning process, the government hopes to reduce planning times and increase public acceptability of renewable energy developments.

Source: *Authors, based on Department of Environment, Land, Water and Planning 2021b; 2021a; 2021c.*

Another ₩2.8 trillion ($221 million) was allocated to the improvement of energy infrastructure, which includes the digital, green, and job security sectors. A sum of ₩1.8 trillion ($144 million) went to renewable energy deployment and the hydrogen economy with the inclusion for construction costs for solar PV for homes, buildings, and public institutions.

When we searched the EPT data on clean conditional and unconditional power generation policies, we found that the policies with descriptions that included our keywords fell into two broad categories: policies aimed at bringing renewable energy to remote communities that are not connected to the main electrical grid and instead rely on nonrenewable energy sources such as diesel, and community-led and community-owed renewable energy projects. As noted in Section 2, policies in these categories are likely to have positive redistributive impacts (i.e., reduce inequality). For this reason, we highlight the policies that fall into these categories.

3.1.1 Remote Communities

Several investments in Canada were directed to bringing renewable energy to remote Indigenous communities that are not connected to the main North American electrical grid and are largely reliant on diesel power generation, which is both expensive (as diesel must be shipped in at high cost) and has negative impacts on local health and the environment (Pembina Institute 2020). In 2021, the federal budget included CAD76.4 million ($57 million) earmarked over three years to build capacity for local renewable energy projects in First Nations, Inuit, and Métis communities and to support feasibility assessment and planning for hydroelectric projects and grid extensions. The government also invested CAD40.5 million ($30.2 million) in the Clarke Lake Geothermal Development Project, which is a wholly owned and Indigenous-led project to build a commercially viable geothermal electricity production facility that can produce between 7 and 15 megawatts and power up to 14,000 households (Natural Resources Canada 2021a). Finally, several community-led projects in the Northwest Territories and Yukon were funded through the Clean Energy for Rural and Remote Communities program, a program that predates the pandemic (Natural Resources Canada 2022). Yukon's government also funded a number of community-based renewable energy projects in its 2020–1 budget (Government of Yukon 2021). In total, the investments for remote communities amounted to $121 million out of a total of $3.3 billion (3.7 percent) for clean conditional and unconditional power generation policies in Canada in the period 2020–1. However, it should also be noted that an unspecified amount of the $1.8 billion allocated to clean power in the Canada Infrastructure Bank Growth Plan (to be delivered through public-private partnerships) is also expected to benefit remote Indigenous communities.

Australia also made two investments in renewable energy in remote communities in 2021. The government allocated AUD19.3 million ($13.4 million) over three years to develop a renewable energy microgrid in the Daintree Rainforest in Far North Queensland. An additional AUD30 million ($21 million) was invested in the Northern Territory's Katherine-Darwin Interconnected System big battery project and microgrid rollout. The project is expected to displace more than 4 million liters of diesel fuel that are consumed in the region each year (Bridge 2022). A sum of AUD15 million ($10.5 million) was allocated to the deployment of renewable energy microgrids in remote Indigenous communities in the Northern Territory. The other AUD15 million ($10.5 million) was invested in a 35 MW battery energy storage system to support the Darwin-to-Katherine grid as more households install rooftop solar (Carroll 2021). These investments amounted to only 1.4 percent of the total spending on clean power generation policies in Australia over 2020–1.

3.1.2 Community-Led and Community-Owned

Spain stands out in the EPT as having an emphasis on citizen participation in renewable energy production. The concept of "energy communities" was introduced in the EU in the Clean Energy for all Europeans legislation in 2019. The EU now has rules to "enable active consumer participation, individually or through citizen energy communities," in renewable energy generation, consumption, sharing and selling, as well as energy storage (European Commission n.d.). In line with this, in 2020, a Royal Decree-Law in Spain was issued that recognizes renewable energy communities as "autonomous legal entities that provide open and voluntary participation" and regulates energy self-consumption in these communities. This framework has allowed renewable energy communities to flourish in the country (Castillo Sánchez 2021).

In the Basque Energy Transition and Climate Change Plan (2021–4, €10.1/$11.5 million) there is discussion of both "citizen energy generation cooperatives," which are designed to "satisfy their own consumption in municipalities in the Basque Country," and promoting other "individual and collective self-consumption projects." The Valencian Community has also allocated aid in 2020 (€550,00/$627,854) and 2021 (€2/$2.3 million) to promote self-consumption in renewable energy communities. For the government of the Valencian Community, local energy communities are considered a "key" element in the transition, since they pursue not only economic ends but also "promote citizen participation, the use of local supply chains and provide employment opportunities, maintaining the value of energy generation within the local population"("Energy Policy Tracker" 2022). In Navarra, a pilot solar project aimed at collective self-consumption will supply a neighborhood located within a radius of 500 meters of the project (€180,000/$205,480). A "citizen community of renewable energy" will be formed, which will be a group of legally constituted users, with voluntary and open participation, which can develop actions for the generation, distribution, supply and consumption of energy, and the provision of different energy services to members (Government of Navarra 2020; "Energy Policy Tracker" 2022).

Outside of Spain, in 2020, New York State allocated $10.6 million to help underserved and disadvantaged communities to access solar energy as part of New York's Social Energy Equity Framework (New York State 2020). In 2021, an additional $52.5 million was allocated for community solar projects to serve up to 50,000 low-to-moderate-income households, affordable housing providers, and facilities serving disadvantaged communities (New York State 2021). These investments comprised 19 percent of the total $332 million that New York State invested in clean power generation in 2020–1.

In Nova Scotia, Canada, a Shared Solar Program was launched in 2021 aimed at reducing barriers to solar adoption for communities and businesses. Under the program, municipalities, First Nation bands, co-ops, and not-for-profits can create community solar gardens. Those renting an apartment can adopt solar energy through a shared ownership or subscription model (Government of Nova Scotia 2021).

Finally, in 2020, Scotland injected £4.5 million ($5.6 million) into the existing Community and Renewable Energy Scheme for local renewable projects (Government of Scotland 2020a). The government has set a target for 2 GW of energy to be produced by community and locally owned energy by 2030.

3.2 Energy Access

Within the countries represented in the EPT, Kenya and Nigeria have the lowest energy access rates (71.4 percent and 55.4 percent respectively, in 2020). Both funded energy access programs during the study period.

3.2.1 Kenya

Approximately, 72 percent of Kenya's population lives in rural areas (World Bank n.d.). As of 2020, 71.4 percent of the population in Kenya had access to electricity, which is a dramatic increase from 2010, when it was only 19.2 percent of the population (World Bank n.d.). However, only 62.7 percent of the rural population has access compared to 94 percent of the urban population. Approximately 13 million people in Kenya continue to lack access to electricity (SEforALL 2020). Kenya has ambitious energy access plans and has set a target to achieve universal electrification by 2022. To achieve this, 5.7 million households will need to be connected to grids, at an estimated cost of $2.3 billion of public investment and $458 million of private investment (Ministry of Energy 2018). Kenya has made immense progress throughout the past decade, expanding electricity access, while at the same time substantially increasing renewable energy production, which now constitutes 78 percent of electricity in Kenya (Ministry of Energy 2021).

Extending the main grid into remote areas is very expensive, so there is an emphasis in Kenya on mini-grid technologies, which are more cost-effective (Nkiriki and Ustun 2017; Blimpo and Cosgrove-Davies 2019). It has been found that most rural populations without access to electricity will be better serviced with mini-grids or stand-alone systems (Kagimu and Ustun 2016).

During the first two years of the pandemic, Kenya had two programs related to energy access. The first, in 2020, involved $4.6 million in credit from the World Bank to provide short-term loans and other forms of financing to off-grid solar companies to enable them to buy stocks of home solar systems and clean cooking stoves (Mwirigi 2020).

In 2021, Kenya launched a project to electrify twenty-two villages through mini-grids in rural Busia County in Northwest Kenya (Takouleu 2021). The mini-grids will incorporate battery backup and range in size from 100 to 60 kWp, with the goal to "expand access to clean, reliable solar power in rural areas [and] pilot delivery of street lighting, water pumping, purification, and appliance financing to ensure that [all] communities and businesses can . . . maximize the health, security, and economic benefits of clean renewable power" (Takouleu 2021). To continue the expansion, a total of $8 million will be required to create 7,000 electricity connections with prepaid solar electricity (InfraCo Africa 2021). A sum of $4.2 million is being provided by InfraCo Africa, and $3.8 million is being provided by the Green Mini-Grid Facility (Takouleu 2021). The project has also received a $235,000 grant from the Private Infrastructure Development Group, which funds InfraCo Africa, to support the various building initiatives and technical studies required for the project. The project is being implemented by Rural Village Energy Solutions (RVE.SOL), a for-profit social entrepreneurship. Although the company's system works on a pay-as-you-go model, they are committed to connecting all households in the communities that they work in, regardless of income (interviews with Lameck Odidah and Stephen Nakholi, 2021).

3.2.2 Nigeria

Nigeria is one of the most populated countries in the world and has the largest economy in Africa, with high levels of poverty and low levels of electricity access (Ogbonnaya et al. 2019). About 85 million Nigerians lack access to electricity (World Bank 2021). As of 2020, 83.9 percent of the urban population and only 24.6 percent of the rural population in Nigeria had access to electricity (World Bank n.d.). It is estimated that Nigeria would have to connect between 500,000 and 800,000 households to the main grid on an annual basis between 2018 and 2030 to achieve SDG 7 (Odin 2018).

Nigeria as a country has access to an abundance of both renewable and nonrenewable energy resources (Nwozor et al. 2021). However, oil remains dominant: around 70 percent of centralized electricity generation is fossil fuel based, with the remaining 30 percent coming from hydro (Akinyele, Belikov, and Levron 2018). The government has been working for decades to expand access with renewable energy, utilizing various policy initiatives. In 2015, the National Renewable Energy and Energy Efficiency Policy created a framework for both on-grid and off-grid solutions (Emodi and Ebele 2016). The National Renewable Action Plan was developed to further the goals laid out in the framework. It included objectives to increase the share of on-grid renewable energy, improve cookstoves, and expand biodiesel (Nwozor et al. 2021). Unfortunately, the implementation of these policies has been slow.

Around 60 percent of Nigeria's citizens cannot access the national power grid, making off-grid systems an attractive option to facilitate economic growth and development (Akinyele and Rayudu 2016). Many of the current mini-grids in use throughout Nigeria are powered from renewable sources, most commonly solar PV (Ekpe and Umoh 2019). As of 2018, there were thirty operating hybrid-solar mini-grids in Nigeria, utilized for the purposes of street lighting, community water pumping, and energy supply to community halls, households, schools, and health centers (Akinyele et al. 2018).

In response to the COVID-19 pandemic, the Government of Nigeria developed a ₦2.3 trillion ($5.6 billion) Economic Sustainability Plan in March 2020 (Government of Nigeria 2020). A sum of N$500 billion ($1.2 million) of this went to the Solar Power Naija Plan (Government of Nigeria 2020). The World Bank and African Finance Development Bank Group have provided a further $765 million in funding. The Solar Power Naija Plan aims to create 5 million solar connections, 250,000 jobs, and impact up to 25 million beneficiaries. As in Kenya, the program is not focused on public provision of electricity, but instead on creating a favorable environment for the private sector to do so (interview with Suleiman Babamanu, 2021). Businesses involved in the project must have at least 70 percent local ownership (SEforALL 2021). Businesses must also demonstrate that they have a plan to source materials from local suppliers (interview with representative of SEforALL, 2021). The focus on localization of the solar power supply chain to develop local manufacturing industries is considered to be one of the most innovative aspects of the Solar Power Naija Plan (ibid) and could, if it is ambitious in scale and ultimately successful, "inspire confidence in the government which would hopefully lead to more investments in those areas" (interview with Chukwumerije Okereke, 2021). However, there is a concern that the emphasis on local production could slow the rollout of the plan and, if the quality of the products is not high, this could damage public confidence in the green transition (interviews with SEforALL and Chukwumerije Okereke, 2021).

The Solar Power Naija Plan may help to overcome one of the major barriers to the deployment of solar PV in Nigeria: the cost. Although these systems can be very cost-effective over time, the upfront cost (up to $400 for an 80 W system) of a solar home system in rural sub-Saharan Africa is too high for many households (Hassan, Morse, and Leach 2020). It remains to be seen whether other barriers will be overcome. For example, there are technological issues to deal with; the capacity of a typical solar home system used in sub-Saharan Africa is also only in the 10–100 W range. Unsurprisingly, many households surveyed both in Federal Capital Territory and Lagos State in Nigeria are unsatisfied with this power capacity, especially in terms of the amount of light provided and the limitations on using a solar system to power appliances (Hassan et al. 2020). Another barrier to the adoption of solar home systems in Nigeria is higher than average system failure rates: a solar electricity system's life span should range from twenty to twenty-five years (Akinyele et al. 2018), but in Nigeria, they commonly fail within two to three years of installation due to poor maintenance (Adeleke 2016).

3.3 Low-Carbon Mobility

The EPT contains information on mobility policies representing commitments of $599 billion. Spending on clean mobility ($292 billion clean conditional, $5.7 billion clean unconditional), and fossil-fueled mobility ($48.2 billion fossil conditional, $240 billion fossil unconditional) was close to equivalent. Figure 5 shows the breakdown of policies by category.

Road construction is a staple of stimulus packages, but this crisis is notable for its impact on the aviation sector and many of the policies reflect this. The International Civil Aviation Organization (2022) reported that the approximate loss of gross passenger operating revenues (compared to 2019 levels) for airlines was approximately $372 billion in 2020 and would be another $324 billion by the end of 2021. Generally, the breadth of the aviation-centered policies – which spanned across all countries listed in the EPT – speaks to the economic dominance of the airline industry. While most airline bailouts were unconditional (see further Greenpeace Europe 2021), France is notable for attaching some "green strings" to its bailout for Air France, including the requirement that it cut domestic flights by 40 percent (Dunn 2020). The country later moved to ban some short haul flights (BBC News 2021).

Some of the other recovery packages for airlines highlight the intricacies of a just recovery in the sector that accommodates equity concerns of marginalized

Clean conditional ■ Clean unconditional ■ Fossil conditional

■ Fossil unconditional ■ Other energy

Figure 5 Public spending on mobility policies by category,
Jan. 2020–Dec. 2021

(**Source:** Authors, based on EPT 2022)

groups. For instance, Canada had the highest number of aviation-related policies, the majority of which were bailout funds. However, the Canadian aviation context is complicated by its expansive geography and the remoteness of many of its communities. For example, the government of Canada committed up to $12 million to support the province of Manitoba to continue essential air travel for remote communities that are otherwise impossible to access. These communities – often located in northern climates – tend to be populated primarily by Indigenous groups, and lack access to medical supplies, food, and equipment for electricity and water systems (Seymour 2020; Transport Canada 2021). Already underserved, these Indigenous communities are reliant on small airlines to ensure individual and community well-being, thus emphasizing the importance of bailing out those fossil-reliant industries during a pandemic. This highlights how equity concerns can complicate the energy transition discourse.

Clean unconditional or conditional energy policies were wide-ranging in focus. While a considerable number of policies addressed public transportation, many of these were funding measures to address shortfalls in revenue due to COVID-19. Policies aimed at decarbonizing public transport generally focused on electrification, such as Poland's commitment to purchase zero-emission busses under its Green Public Transport program, and Canada's efforts to purchase electric school busses in several provinces. The largest single investment in mobility in any category was the $65 billion allocated to public transportation under the US

Bipartisan Infrastructure Law (enacted as the Infrastructure Investment and Jobs Act), representing 22 percent of total clean conditional mobility funding captured in the EPT. This is the largest investment in public transit in US history, yet was still only about one-fifth of the investment made in highways (Lovaas 2022). The investment has equity aspects that are discussed in Section 3.3.1.

Many policies aimed to promote EVs for individual consumption and to build out the infrastructure to support them. Electric vehicle policies centered around removing financial barriers to personal EV purchases by subsidizing their cost, offering incentives, or specifically supporting battery manufacturing. Policies in two Canadian provinces – Nova Scotia and Prince Edward Island – specifically mention that purchases of used EVs are eligible for rebates. This is viewed as an effort to make these programs more equitable (Sharpe and Bauer 2021). California's EV rebate program was targeted to low-income households and is discussed in Section 3.3.2.

Policies relating to infrastructure often complemented these initiatives, with the majority focused on increasing the accessibility of EV charging stations, primarily in cities, but also in some rural areas. The US Bipartisan Infrastructure Law included a set-aside for grants for EV infrastructure in rural communities, as well as low- and moderate-income neighborhoods (US Department of Transportation 2022). New Jersey's program, which specifically targets electric charging infrastructure and other mobility programs to "environmental justice communities across the state," is discussed in Section 3.3.3.

Active transport policies captured in the EPT included expansion of bike and walking pathways, as well as policies that actively reduced the speed and volume of car traffic. New Zealand's commitment, through various funds, to significantly expand a series of walking/cycling trails across the country is an interesting example of an effort not only to encourage active transport (particularly as a form of tourism) but also to better connect rural areas (Government of New Zealand 2020b). Although major cities in the Global North, particularly London, Paris and New York, are frequently cited as cities that utilized the pandemic to rapidly shift to active modes of transportation (see further Duranton 2021), cities in the Global South also invested in cycling and pedestrian infrastructure. One such project in Medellín, Colombia, is an example of an attempted "holistic" low-carbon mobility transition that incorporates justice and equity objectives and is discussed in Section 3.3.4.

3.3.1 United States

Descriptions from the US government of the public transit investments in the Bipartisan Infrastructure Law include numerous references to underserved and marginalized communities. However, in many cases, it is simply assumed that improving transit will benefit these communities because they are more likely to use transit. One program that was specifically targeted to improving equity is the All Stations Accessibility Program, established with $1.75 billion to help finance upgrades to rail transportation that would make them more accessible to people with disabilities, including those who use wheelchairs (Federal Transit Administration 2021). Funding for the preexisting Tribal Transit Program, which supports public transit projects that will meet the growing needs of rural and tribal communities, was also increased (US Department of Transportation 2022).

3.3.2 California

In September 2021, the Governor of California Guy Newson announced a package of over $15 billion in climate measures, including $3.9 billion directed to Zero-Emission Vehicle programs. Funding for 1,000 zero-emission drayage trucks, 1,000 zero-emission school buses and 1,000 transit buses, along with associated charging infrastructure, with projects that "benefit disadvantaged communities" getting priority (State of California 2021). Additionally, funding was directed to the Clean Vehicle Rebate Program (CVRP), which provides up to $4,500 toward the purchase of eligible plug-in hybrid, battery electric, or fuel cell EVs for residents that "meet income requirements" (California Air Resources Board n.d.). An additional $2,500 is available to individuals with household incomes of less than or equal to 400 percent of the federal poverty level. The rebate could also be stacked with the preexisting Clean Vehicle Assistance Program that has a stated objective to prioritize "communities that are disproportionately impacted by pollution," which "often includes low-income communities and communities of color" (Clean Vehicle Assistance Program n.d.), although this program ran out of funds in 2021. Another program – Clean Cars For All – provides up to $9,500 toward an EV to owners of vehicles older than 2005 if they turn over that vehicle (California Air Resources Board n.d.).

Although these programs have equity criteria, concerns have been raised about how accessible they are to those with the greatest need and the CVRP has not "had significant success reaching residents in priority communities" (DeShazo and Di Filippo 2021). For example, it is only possible to apply for the CVRP after purchasing a car, while most low-income buyers need assistance to afford a down payment (Aoun 2022). The rebate is also not available for purchases of used vehicles. Experts have recommended changes in these aspects as well as increasing the rebate and lowering the income cap (DeShazo and Di Filippo 2021).

3.3.3 New Jersey, United States

Transportation is the most polluting sector in New Jersey. It emits nearly half of the state's GHG emissions and is the largest contributor of local air pollution that causes a host of health threats. Low-income and minority populations are disproportionately burdened by air pollution from transportation because they tend to live along transportation corridors (Davis 2021).

In February 2021, Governor Phil Murphy announced an investment of more than $100 million (drawn from proceeds from the New Jersey's participation in the Regional Greenhouse Gas Initiative and its prosecution of Volkswagen for cheating on vehicle emission testing) in transportation projects. The governor also established the Office of Climate Action and the Green Economy which would prioritize "equity and environmental justice." Projects funded within the $100 million package included $9 million in grants for local government electrification of garbage and delivery trucks; $13 million in grants for electric school and shuttle buses in low- and moderate-income communities; $5 million in grants for equitable mobility projects that will bring electric vehicle ride hailing and charging stations to four New Jersey towns and cities; $15 million for electric public buses; and $36 million for electrification of medium- and heavy-duty equipment in port and industrial areas to reduce diesel and black carbon emissions in "environmental justice communities" (New Jersey Office of the Governor 2021). In terms of charging infrastructure, it is notable that grants were made available to encourage installation in multiunit dwellings, with "overburdened communities" eligible for larger grants (New Jersey Board of Public Utilities 2021). A law was also passed requiring multifamily developments with more than five units to reserve 15 percent of parking spaces to be made ready for a charging station and for these to be installed within six years (New Jersey Department of Community Affairs 2021).

In addition to the $36 million investment, in December 2021, the New Jersey Department of Environmental Protection adopted the Advanced Clean Trucks rule, first developed in California, which requires manufacturers to sell an increasing number of zero-emission trucks in New Jersey beginning in 2025, with 40–75 percent of new truck sales required to be zero-emission by 2035 (Environmental Defense Fund 2021). The rule is considered particularly important for reducing health risks from pollution from diesel trucks for lower-income families and marginalized communities living near freight corridors, ports, bus depots, and Newark airport (Environmental Defense Fund n.d.). However, environmental justice advocates are pushing for the state to also adopt stricter emissions standards to reduce pollution levels faster (Tigue 2022).

3.3.4 Medellín, Colombia

Medellín's eco-city project, led by Mayor Daniel Quintero, seemingly takes a holistic, structural approach to transitioning the city's mobility systems to low-carbon transport, by emphasizing electrified public transit and increased bicycle and walking pathways. The project aims to "cut carbon emissions by 20 percent, electrify all public transport by 2030, expand bike lanes by 50 percent, and double the number of public transport lines" (Glatsky 2021). The initiative is based on existing green infrastructure: in January 2021, Medellín opened new electric charging stations for its sixty-nine electric busses (Glatsky 2021); it also already boasts a city-led, award-winning "green corridor" project which planted trees along streets to cool the city down (Moloney 2021). Another part of the eco-city project is to source its electric buses domestically, rather than continuing to purchase them from China (Glatsky 2021).

The eco-city project appears to aim to fundamentally restructure how individuals move, rather than emphasizing private forms of green transit. The city website states that it hopes to "Establish the foundations of the ecological transition to direct Medellín to a future of sustainability, where the full enjoyment of the right to the city, the dignified habitability of its inhabitants and the functional and harmonious integration of rural areas is guaranteed through the recognition and access to the rights of rural people" (City of Medellín 2020).

However, there has been significant opposition to the project from current and former city council members, including one from the "left-leaning Green Alliance party" (Glatsky 2021). This opposition stems primarily from the fact that Medellín's city council cut its environmental budget earlier in 2021, making its claims for an "eco-city" seem suspect and unrealistic (Glatsky 2021). Environmental activists in Medellín are also wary of the project, given that Medellín's city council has undergone significant membership changes recently, wherein politicians with the requisite environmental knowledge to implement an "eco-city" project have been replaced with Quintero's political allies (Glatsky 2021). One interviewee pointed out that there has been significant political overhaul that will likely impact the viability of this type of initiative, stating that there were originally "a lot of people in the mayor's administration who … were really knowledgeable and had experience … [but have been] replaced by people that … didn't have any expertise" (interview with Genevieve Glatsky, 2021).

Ultimately, Medellín's eco-city initiative is still in its initial phases, and it is unclear whether it will bring about the type of structural changes to mobility systems that are needed for a green and just recovery.

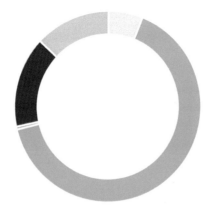

Clean conditional ▪ Clean unconditional ▪ Fossil conditional
▪ Fossil unconditional ▪ Other energy

Figure 6 Public spending on building energy policies by category
Jan. 2020–Dec. 2021
(**Source:** Authors, based on EPT 2022)

3.4 Energy-Efficient Buildings

The EPT contains information on 197 policies related to buildings worth $61.2 billion. Only nine policies in five countries (Finland, France, Poland, Turkey, and Ukraine) were fossil conditional or unconditional and a further seven policies were classified as "other energy." Most of these policies were aimed at either switching heating systems from oil to gas or reducing energy costs, although Turkey's $9.4 billion to provide low-interest home and home renovation loans was designated "fossil unconditional" based on the fact that it had no energy efficiency conditions attached and China's $7.8 billion renovation program was classified as "other energy" because the amount that would be directed to clean energy is unquantified. Several of these policies were designated as negative in value, because they represented loss of tax income rather than provisioning of new funds (these values are not included in the total funding cited earlier in this section).

A sum of $43.5 billion (71 percent) was committed to clean conditional and unconditional policies related to buildings (see Figure 6). However, a small number of countries dominate: the United Kingdom (including policies in Scotland and Wales) accounts for 27.4 percent of this total, Canada for 19.5 percent, and France for 17.6 percent. While $43.5 billion may seem like a significant sum, to put this into context, the Pembina Institute has estimated that in Canada alone public investments in building retrofits of 10–$15 billion per year, every year between now and 2040, are required to meet the country's climate targets (Frappé-Sénéclauze 2021).

Policy descriptions in the EPT for programs in Canada, New Zealand, the United Kingdom, and the United States explicitly mention poverty, social housing, or low-income households and are therefore discussed in further detail. The Korean Green New Deal also mentioned that "insulation system will be replaced with high performance ones in 225,000 public rental housings that are over 15 years old" but no additional information on this program was available (in English) at the time of writing.

3.4.1 Canada

In 2017, space heating accounted for 63 percent of Canada's GHG emissions from buildings (NRCAN 2019). Heating and cooling of buildings accounts for 17 percent of Canada's total GHG emissions (Energy and Mines Ministers' Conference and Natural Resources Canada 2017).

To address building efficiency, the federal government launched the Canada Greener Homes Grant in May 2021. This retrofit program targeted toward homeowners has a budget of CAD2.6 billion ($1.8 billion) over seven years. Homeowners can access a maximum of CAD600 ($477) as a reimbursement for home energy audits and up to CAD5000 ($3,976) in reimbursement for eligible retrofits (Natural Resources Canada 2021b). This program has been critiqued as being likely to only incentivize one-off retrofits rather than deep retrofits and to be primarily taken up by middle and upper-income households.

The 2021 budget also allocated CAD778.7 million ($619 million) annually for a total of five years in interest-free loans for deep retrofits worth up to CAD40,000 ($31,812). Brendan Haley, Policy Director at Efficiency Canada, estimates that deep energy retrofits in Canada range from CAD40,000 to 100,000 ($31,812–$79,530) (interview, 2021) and that this program is therefore not likely to strongly incentivize such efforts. The loan program includes a dedicated stream for low-income homeowners and rentals, including not-for-profit and low-income housing. However, according to Tom-Pierre Frappé-Sénéclauze, the Director for Buildings and Urban Solutions at the Pembina Institute, the loan program still essentially targets upper-middle-class house-holds who had previously considered retrofitting their home, and so is not accessible to households with less spending capacity (interview, 2021). Upper-middle-class property owners are more than likely to already have access to low interest rate financing from their bank or credit union (Frappé-Sénéclauze 2021). Haley (2020) concurs, noting that "Lower income Canadians will either not qualify or will be reluctant to participate due to already high levels of personal debt."

There are also geographic inequalities that have been taken into consideration in the design of the Greener Home Grant program, but possibly not sufficiently. The program includes specific funding for northern and off-grid communities. Normally, homeowners must prove that they own and primarily reside in the building receiving the grant; however, in the territories, Nunavik, Nunatsiavut, and off-grid communities, the criteria differ (NRCAN 2021). Indigenous people represent most of the population in Northern Canada, and constantly see challenges in the realm of adequate housing (Nicol, Segel-Brown, and Mohamed Ahmed 2021). The Canada Greener Homes Grant makes an exception to the primary residence criteria in order to allow Indigenous governments to access the grant. However, challenges remain, particularly with booking the home energy evaluations that must be completed prior to any retrofits. The Northwest Territories, for example, only has one company that conducts home energy evaluations (Whitehouse 2021). In 2021, the wait time to receive an evaluation there was between six months to a year (Whitehouse 2021).

3.4.2 New Zealand

In May 2020, the Government of New Zealand announced a NZD56 million ($37 million) boost to an existing insulation and heating program called Warmer Kiwi Homes. The Energy and Resources Minister Megan Woods made an explicit connection to the pandemic, noting that "insulation and heating helps to prevent respiratory illness" and also highlighted that the program was targeted to help "the most vulnerable people in our communities" (Government of New Zealand 2020a). The program was initially launched in 2018, with NZD142.5 million ($93.4 million) allocated over four years. To be eligible for a grant, homeowners either needed to have a Community Services Card or lived in an area identified as low-income. Low-income areas are determined using the New Zealand Deprivation Index. The original aim was to insulate or install a heater in 52,000 houses but the bump in funding allows for 9,000 additional houses; the grants now cover 90 percent of the cost of getting insulation or a heater installed (up from the previous 67 percent), with the grant for heaters capped at NZD3000 ($1,966).

In a study of 127 households that received an energy-efficient heat pump in the program, 82 percent said their house was much more comfortable or more comfortable after having received it and the proportion of households that reported ever having restricted heating due to cost fell from 80 percent to 21 percent (Fyfe et al. 2022).

Several policies in the United Kingdom are relevant to this discussion. One that is directly focused on low-income households is the Social Housing Decarbonisation Fund, which began in 2020–1 as a £50 million ($63 million) demonstration project. There are approximately 4.0 million social homes in England (17 percent of all homes). Social housing is generally more efficient than other types of homes in England, but it still accounts for around 23 percent of households experiencing energy poverty (Department for Business, Energy & Industrial Strategy 2021). The Social Housing Decarbonisation Fund was established to help social housing landlords improve the least energy-efficient rented social homes. In the demonstration phase, over 2,300 homes were improved and at least 1,300 local jobs were supported. A further £179 million ($225 million) in funding was provided for Wave 1 of the program in 2020–1 and £800 million ($1 billion) has been confirmed for Wave 2, which will run for three years from 2022 (Department for Business, Energy & Industrial Strategy 2022). The funds will be directed to upgrades of 50,000 households in social housing with insulation, heat pumps, and solar panels. The government expects to help households in England and Scotland save up to £450 ($566) a year on their energy bills and to support around 8,000 green jobs annually.

The largest programs launched in the United Kingdom during the pandemic to address building energy efficiency were the £1 billion ($1.3 billion) for local authority retrofitting schemes and the £2 billion ($2.5 billion) Green Homes Grant to retrofit private homes, introduced in the July 2020 Plan for Jobs. A sum of £1.5 billion ($1.9 billion) of the Green Homes program was to be dispersed through a voucher system that households could apply for directly, while the remaining £500 million ($629 million) went to a Local Authority Delivery program focused on low-income households (social housing tenants and low-income families) (Committee of Public Accounts 2021; Department for Business, Energy & Industrial Strategy 2021). The vouchers could cover up to two-thirds of the cost of a variety of low-carbon heating options or energy efficiency improvements. The government aimed to make 650,000 homes more energy efficient, save households up to £300 ($377) a year on their bills, cut carbon by more than half a megatonne per year, and support around 140,000 green jobs. The Green Homes Grant started in September but by February 2021, only around 22,000 vouchers had been issued, and fewer than 3,000 installations had been completed. The scheme was scrapped in March 2021. Of the total spending (£264 million/$332 million) by March 2021, £211 million ($265 million) flowed to low-income households (Hinson and Adcock 2021).

The main flaw in the program was that it provided a very short window (six months) for vouchers to be used and the retrofit industry simply did not have capacity to complete such a large volume of installations, so applicants were unable to find an approved contractor (Hodgkin and Sasse 2021). The prioritization of the stimulus effect of a short program that could provide a significant economic boost was at the expense of workers, many of whom suffered from the scheme because they invested time and money in accreditation only then to see the program canceled (Climate Change Committee 2021). Following the end of the program, a government committee advised that short-term programs are not suitable either to create jobs and support the industry or to achieve net-zero targets and that what is needed is a "stable, long-term plan" (Committee of Public Accounts 2021).

In the wake of the collapse of the program, a protest group specifically focused on energy efficiency in homes formed in the United Kingdom. Insulate Britain has two main demands of the government: that it should fund the insulation of all social housing by 2025 and that it should develop a "legally-binding national plan" for a low energy and low-carbon retrofit of all homes in Britain by 2030 (Insulate Britain n.d.). With the outbreak of war in the Ukraine and an ensuing energy crisis in Europe, the United Kingdom was the hardest hit and public pressure forced the government to responded with a new £6 billion fund for insulation and replacing gas boilers with heat pumps in November 2022 (Lawson 2022).

3.4.4 United States

On November 15, 2021, as part of the Bipartisan Infrastructure Law, $3.5 billion was allocated to budget for the Weatherization Assistance Program (WAP) for a five-year period. This is a long-standing Department of Energy program rather than a new initiative. Congress created WAP in 1976 under Title IV of the *Energy Conservation and Production Act*. It is funded through federal appropriations that have averaged between $100 million and $450 million annually. In 2009, it received a massive influx of $4.7 billion under Obama's stimulus package (in response to the GFC). The program is specifically targeted to provide energy efficiency upgrades in low-income households. The program has been extensively evaluated, particularly following the large injection of funds during the Obama administration. Researchers found that 340,158 units were retrofitted under the program in 2010 at a cost of $2.3 billion ($2 billion of which came from WAP) and the cost to weatherize a unit was $6,812 on average (Tonn et al. 2015).

During the GFC stimulus-funded period, the WAP supported approximately 28,000 jobs (directly and indirectly) and increased national economic output by

$4 billion. However, many of these jobs were temporary, with 25 percent of auditors, 27 percent of crew chiefs, and 40 percent of crew members leaving the field of low-income weatherization only two years after their initial involvement in the WAP (Tonn et al. 2015). In terms of environmental impacts, carbon emissions declined by an estimated 7.3 MMT CO_2-e (Tonn et al. 2015). There were also health and social benefits of the program. The Oak Ridge National Laboratory study valued these at $3.8 billion in 2010 or $14,148 per household (Tonn et al. 2015). While some have critiqued the program for not being cost-effective (Fowlie, Greenstone, and Wolfram 2015), others stress that the program has numerous nonenergy retrofits, like the removal of asbestos and mold (Detrow 2015; Plumer 2015). These retrofits are also done to improve the comfort of low-income households, for example by allowing people to heat their homes more in the winter without increasing their energy bills. Programs like WAP are done "for equity reasons and social service reasons as much as savings" (Nadel quoted in Detrow 2015). Similarly, Kushler (2015) argues that the GHG emissions reduction benefits "are just a bit of frosting on the benefits cake. No one would suggest WAP should be considered as entirely, or even primarily, a mechanism to fight climate change."

3.5 Support for Fossil Fuel–Dependent Communities

The EPT only contains a handful of policies that included an element of worker training. The state government of Queensland in Australia invested $12 million in the Pinkenba Renewable Energy Training Facility. The facility will provide pre-trade apprenticeships and post-trade courses for up to 300 electrician students at a time and support forty teaching positions (Peacock 2021). In Canada, several of the federal government's investments in remote communities (discussed in Section 3.1.1) included training opportunities for members of Indigenous communities. The Optimized Retrofit Programme in Wales also included some job training elements. In the United States, the Bipartisan Infrastructure Law provided $55 million in grant funding in 2022 to train transit workers to use zero-emission vehicles "to ensure that diesel mechanics and other transit workers are not left behind in the transition to new technology" (US Department of Transportation 2022).

In terms of policies more specifically concerned with communities that have traditionally been dependent on the fossil fuel industry for employment, there are interesting examples of worker-focused policies in Europe. In Germany, the Coal Phase Out Act was passed on July 3, 2020. Alongside the law, €40 billion ($43 billion) has been allocated to support the economic transformation of coal regions, including up to €5 billion ($5.4 billion) by 2048 for adaptation payments for older workers in lignite mines and hard coal and lignite power plants who lose their jobs in the coal phaseout. However, the final plan did not include any targeted education and training for coal workers who were not ready to retire, despite the fact that this was recommended by a multi-stakeholder "Coal Commission" that was tasked with providing guidance for the legislation (Raitbaur 2021). On the other hand, the EU- and Scotland-funded programs that were directly aimed at retraining workers impacted by the transition away from fossil fuels are discussed further in Sections 3.5.1 and 3.5.2. Funding programs in Canada and the United States that address oil and gas well and coal mine reclamation (categorized as "fossil conditional" in the EPT) are summarized in Sections 3.5.3 and 3.5.4.

3.5.1 European Union

The EU released a proposal for a Just Transition Mechanism in January 2020 as part of the European Green Deal (European Commission 2020a). The Just Transition Mechanism provides financial and accountability tools that help address the transition and help unlock the mobilization of funds, particularly of regions and communities most exposed to high employment in fossil fuel production or with GHG-intensive industries. EU member states are expected to develop national just transition plans, commit 30 percent of their recovery spending to net-zero transition, and co-finance/match funding requirements by the European Commission.

The Just Transition Fund is one pillar of the mechanism that will be directed to efforts to "alleviate the socio-economic costs triggered by climate transition," including "up- and reskilling of workers, job-search assistance and active inclusion of jobseekers programmes" (European Commission 2020a). The European Commission's initial January 2020 proposal had a budget of €40 billion ($40.6 billion), but only €17.5 billion ($17.8 billion) was approved by the European Council in December 2020. Those countries that have the largest anticipated job losses (Poland, Germany, Romania, and Czech Republic) will be allocated the largest amount of funds. Countries will have to provide matching funding of €1.5–3 for every euro from the Fund (European Commission 2020a). It has been argued that because the fund is small, it should be targeted exclusively to social support and worker retraining efforts (Cameron et al. 2020; World Resources Institute 2021b).

3.5.2 Scotland

Between 2014 and 2017, the United Kingdom's oil and gas sector lost 150,000 jobs due to a sharp downturn in oil prices (World Resources Institute 2021a). The impacts of this were the worst in Scotland. As of 2019, the sector employed

86,000 people (Palmer 2022). Although the renewable energy sector is growing in Scotland, it employed only 22,600 people in the same year (Black 2021).

In the fall of 2020, the Scottish Government launched the National Training Transition Fund (NTTF) and awarded £25 million ($31 million) to Skills Development Scotland, several colleges and universities, Scottish Enterprise, Lantra, and Creative Scotland (Government of Scotland 2020b). Unlike its predecessor, the Transition Training Fund (TTF), which ran from 2017 to 2019, the NTTF was not exclusively focused on oil and gas workers (European Commission 2020b). However, the government emphasized that it would be "targeted towards the most exposed sectors including oil and gas, aviation and tourism" (Government of Scotland 2020b). The success of the TTF, which helped 4,272 oil and gas workers, also informed the development of the NTTF (World Resources Institute 2021). The goal of the NTTF is to "boost the supply of skills in areas such as sustainable green jobs and raise the profile of training opportunities linked to Scotland's transition to a net zero economy" (Government of Scotland 2020b). In the first year of the program, 6,000 individuals were supported. A second phase launched in 2021 aims to provide more than 20,000 additional training opportunities (Government of Scotland 2021).

In addition to the NTTF, the government launched the North East Economic Recovery and Skills Fund in 2021 to help address the impacts of both the pandemic and the downturn in the oil and gas industry in the Northeast region of Scotland (Government of Scotland 2022). The fund includes projects managed by the Energy Transition Zone in Aberdeen, which provides on-the-job transition training in the renewable energy sector and upskilling of oil and gas sector employees (Skills Development Scotland 2021).

3.5.3 Canada

Across Canada there are hundreds of thousands of inactive and abandoned oil and gas wells. Canada's COVID Economic Response plan included CAD1.72 billion ($1.37 billion) in funding for well cleanup (Department of Finance Canada 2020). Much of the funding has flowed to cleaning up "inactive wells," which are those that are still owned by viable companies that could fund the well cleanup themselves. Wells are considered "orphaned" if "there is no known, financially viable operator capable of addressing the environmental liabilities" associated with closure (Parliamentary Budget Office 2022). Wells are designated as "abandoned" if they "do not have a solvent owner and require cleanup in the form of either plugging and/or reclamation but have yet to transition to orphan status" (Parliamentary Budget Office 2022).

The largest portion of funds went to Alberta (CAD1 billion/$800 million) (which had lobbied heavily for the program – see Corkal 2021), with the remainder divided between Saskatchewan (CAD400 million/$318 million), British Columbia ($120 million/$95 million), and as a loan to the Orphan Well Association in Alberta and in British Columbia ($200 million/$159 million) (Ramsay 2020). No funding was provided to Ontario, even though the wells in the province are some of the oldest in North America, dating as far back as the 1800s, meaning the businesses that created them are near impossible to trace (Jeffords 2021). Minister Chrystia Freeland defended the decision to leave Ontario out of the program, asserting that the program should be concentrated in the energy-producing provinces (Ensing 2021).

Indigenous leaders in Canada have been lobbying since the orphan wells program was announced to receive an allotment of funding. There is funding needed to clean up oil and gas wells on First Nations and Métis land in Alberta (Bakx 2020). The Indian Resource Council requested to receive 10 percent of Alberta's funds and although it took half a year, the provincial government eventually agreed. A sum of CAD85 million ($68 million) will be allocated toward First Nations land and CAD15 million ($12 million) toward Métis land in Alberta. This will allow Indigenous communities to have control over the gas sites that will be cleaned up. In addition, Indigenous-owned companies have received CAD1.5 million ($1.2 million) in Saskatchewan (Bakx 2020).

While the cleanup of any oil and gas wells would be welcomed in the communities in which they are situated, experts have expressed concern that the program will set a dangerous precedent of leaving taxpayers on the hook for costs that should be borne by oil and gas producers (De Souza and Wong 2020). The key issue, as pointed out by the Parliamentary Budget Office (2022), is that "nearly half the funding in Alberta has been disbursed to firms that are viable." The Center for International Environmental Law (2021) notes that "Because the grants are distributed not according to an operator's inability to pay, but based on their overall liability, the producers with the biggest environmental footprints get the largest checks."

The Government of Alberta has taken some steps to address the concern that public money should not be spent on cleaning up the industry's mess. Oil and gas companies will be required to spend CAD422 million ($336 million) on cleanup and remediation in 2022 and CAD443 million ($352 million) in 2023, with the amount continuing to increase each year. While this is a positive development, the Parliamentary Budget Office (2022) estimates that the amount Alberta is requiring the industry to provide is insufficient and that the funding gap will grow to CAD642 million ($511 million) by 2025 if additional finance is not secured.

3.5.4 United States

The 2021 Bipartisan Infrastructure Law included $11.3 billion for the Abandoned Mine Land (AML) program (Department of the Interior 2022d) and $4.7 billion for orphaned well site plugging, remediation, and restoration activities (Department of the Interior 2022c).

Over a period of eleven years, the AML program will provide grants to eligible states and Tribes for projects that "close dangerous mine shafts, reclaim unstable slopes, prevent releases of harmful gases, including methane, improve water quality by treating acid mine drainage and restore water supplies damaged by mining" (Department of the Interior 2022d). Pennsylvania, which is home to a third of the abandoned mine lands in the United States, was eligible for the most funding in 2022 (nearly $245 million), followed by West Virginia, Illinois, Kentucky, and Ohio (Groom 2022). The United States has, since 1977, required companies to reclaim abandoned mining sites. It also has a system where active coal companies pay a per-ton fee into a fund to clean up sites that were abandoned prior to 1977 (Just Transition Fund n.d.). However, the funding is insufficient and as the amount of coal mined in the United States falls, so too does the funding available for reclamation (Groom 2022; Just Transition Fund n.d).

In May 2022, the Department of Interior (Department of the Interior 2022b) released draft guidance on the implementation of the AML program. The guidance contains many elements that indicate a strong potential for the program to contribute to a just transition. The draft guidance instructs states and Tribes to prioritize projects that provide employment opportunities to current and former employees of the coal industry; prioritize projects that are beneficial to disadvantaged communities and support the revitalization of such communities to meet the overall objectives of Justice40 (a Biden administration initiative that aims to "deliver at least 40 percent of the overall benefits from Federal investments in climate and clean energy to disadvantaged communities" – see Young, Mallory, and McCarthy 2021); require contractors to support safe, equitable, and fair labor practices by adopting collective bargaining agreements, local hiring provisions (as applicable), project labor agreements, and community benefits agreements; and incorporate input from disadvantaged communities of color, low-income communities, and Tribal and Indigenous communities into the selection of projects to be funded. Moreover, applicants will be required to provide detail in their proposals on how environmental justice issues within coalfield communities will be addressed; how any disproportionate burden of adverse human health or environmental effects of coal AML problems on disadvantaged communities, communities of color, low-income communities, and Tribal and Indigenous communities will be identified and addressed; and whether and to what extent the proposed projects will reduce GHG emissions, particularly methane emissions. Finally, in contrast to the previous AML program, the draft guidance requires that workers be paid prevailing wages (as determined by the Secretary of Labor in accordance with the Davis–Bacon Act), which will ensure that contractors do not reduce wages in order to win contracts (Appalachian Voices 2022).

The program and draft guidance for its implementation have been widely praised. Chelsea Barnes, the Legislative Director for Appalachian Voices (a nonprofit focused on advocating for a healthy environment and just economy in the Appalachian region) applauded the prioritization of Justice40 and encouraged the DOI "to collaborate with stakeholders to ensure that this abandoned mine land funding is reaching the most disadvantaged communities" (Appalachian Voices 2022). Eric Dixon, Senior Researcher with Ohio River Valley Institute, argues that the draft guidance "signals a shift toward prioritizing the reclamation workers – from backhoe operators to field scientists – who make mine cleanup possible" although he also wished to see even stronger wording in the final version (Appalachian Voices 2022).

The final guidance for the $4.7 billion orphaned well cleanup program was released in April 2022 and like the AML program, it reflects some of the principles of the Justice40 Initiative. In the "recommended" (not required) section of the guidance, states are asked to provide details of how they will "identify and address any disproportionate burden of adverse human health or environmental effects of orphaned wells on communities of color, low-income communities, and Tribal and Indigenous communities"; any "Training programs, registered apprenticeships, and local and economic hire agreements for workers"; plans to "support opportunities for all workers, including workers underrepresented in well plugging or site remediation, to be trained and placed in good-paying jobs directly related to the project"; and plans "to incorporate equity for underserved communities into their planning, including supporting the expansion of high-quality, good paying jobs through workforce development programs and incorporating workforce strategy into project development" (Department of the Interior 2022a). The payment of prevailing wages is a requirement.

While environmental groups and policy experts have generally welcomed the development of the fund, many have expressed similar concerns to those raised in Canada, that is, that not enough is being done to ensure that the oil and gas industry is held accountable for cleaning up their own mess (Biven 2022; Kretzmann and others 2022). The amount of funding is also likely to be insufficient to tackle the problem. It has been estimated that it could cost

$280 billion to close over 2.6 million documented unplugged onshore wells in the United States that are at risk of being orphaned (Carbon Tracker 2020). Since the announcement of the funding, the number of documented orphaned wells (always known to be a substantial underestimate of the true number) has exploded, and some are concerned that states will be incentivized to bail out negligent operators (Sadasivam 2022).

3.6 Summary

In terms of the "greenness" of the COVID-19 stimulus, our findings – that an insufficient proportion of investment (arguably, 100 percent of stimulus should be green) was directed to projects that would facilitate decarbonization – are consistent with other studies. However, clearly the greenness of stimulus does vary across areas of energy policy. Policies directed to buildings are predominantly in the clean categories, whereas there is close to an even split between fossil fuel and clean policies in the case of power generation and mobility investments. However, even in the buildings category, the total amount of green investment is far below what is considered necessary for a rapid energy transition.

With respect to the justice dimension of the recovery, it is evident that this has not been prioritized in the vast majority of policies tracked in the EPT. There is substantial scope for governments to improve both the efficacy of their green policies and to address inequality through more targeting to low-income and other marginalized groups. A small number of policies highlighted in this section could serve as models for future government programs, although more detailed studies are merited.

4 Conclusions

This Element has explored energy policies, in five key areas, adopted by governments during the COVID-19 pandemic that have the potential to reduce both GHGs and inequality. Previous assessments of the greenness of the COVID-19 recovery have concluded that governments have failed to seize the opportunity to accelerate the energy transition through stimulus measures targeted at decarbonization. We concur with these assessments. Our research adds to the overall picture that most of the green stimulus measures adopted in the period January 2020–December 2021 did not prioritize ensuring that the energy transition would be a just one. Nevertheless, we have also highlighted that in some sectors, and in some jurisdictions, issues of justice are being taken seriously and are being actively integrated into energy policies. The implementation of these policies and their impacts, in terms of reducing emissions and benefiting marginalized groups, are worthy of follow-up studies.

Investments in renewable energy have great potential to contribute to a just transition, but the mode of deployment will determine the extent to which they deliver benefits beyond GHG emissions reductions. There appears to be growing interest in community-led and community-owned models of renewable energy generation, particularly in Europe. While it cannot be assumed that such approaches will work in every context, or will deliver just outcomes for all community members, this does appear to be an overall positive development. Similarly, investments for remote communities in Australia and Canada, while small compared to overall spending on renewable energy, have potential to deliver significant benefits to communities currently reliant on dirty forms of energy such as diesel.

Renewable energy also has great potential to deliver equity outcomes in countries that currently lack universal energy access. Off-grid technologies like mini-grids and solar home systems can reduce poverty and improve public health while reducing GHG emissions. The pandemic-era programs in Kenya and Nigeria could help to demonstrate the viability of the off-grid sector and provide a model for other countries within the sub-Saharan Africa region (interview with representative of SEforALL, 2021). However, given the problems that many countries have faced with the provision of basic services by the private sector, more research on these cases is warranted.

In terms of the mobility sector, there has been a missed opportunity with public investments in 2020–1 to advance distributive justice. Although there are examples of cities that have seized the opportunity presented by the pandemic to try to upend the car-focused model of urban life, a substantial amount of green stimulus in transportation still flowed to supporting EV purchases by middle- and upper-income earners. As Brand et al. (2021, 2) argue, "there is growing consensus that technological substitution via electrification will not be sufficient or fast enough to transform the transport system." Thus, the overwhelming focus on EV expansion, to the extent that it diverts attention and investments from the public transportation and active transportation sectors, is not justified. Furthermore, very few jurisdictions have made any attempt to target EV subsidies to low-income households even though such an approach would provide greater policy efficacy in addition to delivering on equity. Governments should provide targeted subsidies, as California has, but ensure that they are accessible (i.e., provided at the point of purchase) and are available for the purchase of used vehicles (as in some Canadian provinces).

When it comes to buildings, the picture is mixed. There are certainly some countries that have prioritized energy-efficient retrofits for low-income households and social housing, particularly the United States and to some extent the United Kingdom, while others (notably, Canada, where heating buildings makes a significant contribution to overall GHG emissions) continue to primarily target middle- and upper-income earners. As energy prices skyrocketed in 2022 (brought on by the war in Ukraine), concerns about energy poverty, even in the rich countries of the Global North, have substantially increased. Protest groups like Insulate Britain have also helped to draw media attention to the issue. Hopefully, these factors will lead to greater emphasis on justice and equity issues in retrofit programs in more countries moving forward.

Finally, some attention was given in the pandemic period to job losses and other harms that have been inflicted on fossil-dependent communities, which is sensible given the degree to which these communities have suffered in recent years. However, the funds that have been offered by governments that will directly support workers and communities are a tiny fraction of that which has been provided to the industry itself in the form of fossil fuel subsidies. Furthermore, it is concerning that reclamation programs that should have positive outcomes in terms of environmental and health improvements may also serve as bailouts for negligent companies. While the United States' plans for mine reclamation and orphaned well cleanup are not without concerns in this regard, they do offer advances in terms of the prioritization of disadvantaged communities and assurances about good conditions for workers. These programs, and others that are implemented in line with the Justice40 initiative, will be important ones for researchers to monitor.

Clearly, much further research in this area is merited. This preliminary review of energy policies adopted in the pandemic period has largely relied on an assessment of governments' proposals for funding. Of course, the actual outcomes of funding programs may diverge substantially from stated objectives. Furthermore, we have not investigated the question of why governments have largely failed to act on the existing evidence that targeting policies to underserved communities and marginalized groups can improve program outcomes by delivering greater GHG emissions reductions as well as additional benefits to society. Is this the result of a lack of awareness among policymakers, or are political factors (e.g., the desire to appease voters in higher-income brackets and those who donate to political campaigns) more important?

Even as restrictions lift and daily life returns to an approximation of "normal," the impacts of COVID-19 continue to be felt and will likely endure long after the pandemic is officially deemed "over." Additional crises have also sparked further calls for government spending. While our study points to a deficient recovery thus far, there remain opportunities for innovative and equitable energy transitions. One example, which falls outside the period that we studied but is worthy of mention, is the US Inflation Reduction Act (IRA) of 2022. It combines the objectives of carbon emission mitigation with industrial policy objectives of creating competitive manufacturing sectors with more secure supply chains. The IRA specifically relies on tax credits and targets renewable energy, low-carbon mobility, energy-efficient buildings, and fossil fuel communities all at once (US Department of Energy 2022). The energy and climate commitments together were estimated at $369 billion at the time the IRA was passed (Senate Democrats 2022), but since some tax credits are uncapped, the eventual value might be much higher (Goldman Sachs 2023).

In terms of renewable energy, tax credits will support the deployment of, or investments in, solar, wind, geothermal, and energy storage infrastructure. Many of the low-carbon electricity tax credits have a bonus (i.e., a higher tax credit) when projects are located in brownfield sites, fossil fuel communities, low-income communities, or on Tribal land.

On the side of low-carbon mobility, EVs are incentivized through a clean vehicle credit that can go up to $7,500 per vehicle depending on where its components come from. The IRA also includes a consumer tax credit for previously owned EVs as well as a credit for new commercial clean vehicles. There is a maximum income eligibility that is supposed to reduce the number of wealthy households that are eligible for tax credits, even if the maximum income cap is still very high.

With respect to building efficiency, the IRA extends a tax credit for residential clean energy, including battery storage, and extends the credit for energy efficiency home improvements. It also adds more money to the Home Energy Performance-Based Whole House Rebates, which is intended to increase funding specifically for low- and moderate-income households. Tax credits are available for energy savings retrofits, but also for heat pumps, electric stoves, and insulation, to name a few.

Finally, the IRA also provides funding for specific community investment and energy justice projects, ranging from environmental and climate justice grants over neighborhood access and equity grants to specific tax credits for reducing air pollution, purchasing clean heavy-duty vehicles, and improving low-emissions electricity projects in lower-income and affected communities. The implementation of the IRA and its impacts will be the subject of important research in the years to come.

Acronyms and Abbreviations

CO_2	carbon dioxide
CVRP	Clean Vehicle Rebate Program (California)
EPT	Energy Policy Tracker
EU	European Union
EV	electric vehicle
GFC	global financial crisis
GHG	greenhouse gas
GWh	gigawatt hours
GT	Gigaton
IEA	International Energy Agency
IISD	International Institute for Sustainable Development
ILO	International Labour Association
IMF	International Monetary Fund
IPCC	Intergovernmental Panel on Climate Change
IRA	Inflation Reduction Act (US)
IRENA	International Renewable Energy Agency
MDB	Multilateral Development Bank
MMT CO_2-e	million metric tons of carbon dioxide equivalents
MW	megawatt
NTTF	National Transition Training Fund (Scotland)
OECD	Organisation for Economic Cooperation and Development
RVE.SOL	Rural Village Energy Solutions
SDG	Sustainable Development Goal
SEforALL	Sustainable Energy for All
TTF	Transition Training Fund (Scotland)
UNEP	United Nations Environment Program
UNFCCC	United Nations Framework Convention on Climate Change
WAP	Weatherization Assistance Program (US)

Appendix

Interviewees

Suleiman Babamanu, Rural Electrification Agency, Nigeria
Anup Bandivadekar, International Council on Clean Transportation
Chris Brodie, Skills Development Scotland
David Coyne, Skills Development Scotland
Megan Egler, Parkland Institute, Canada
Tom-Pierre Frappé-Sénéclauze, Pembina Institute, Canada
Genevieve Glatsky, Al Jazeera
Ana Guerra Marin, Iron & Earth, Canada
Dr. Brendan Haley
Gerard Hendriksen, GMG Kenya
Oliver Massmann, Duane Morris
Stephen Nakholi, RVE.SOL
Lameck Odidah, RVE.SOL
Prof. Chuks Okereke, Alex Ekwueme Federal University Ndufu-Alike Nigeria
Ashwini Swain, The Center for Policy Research, India
Bruce Wilson, Iron & Earth, Canada
SEforAll

Note: only those interviewees that did not wish to remain anonymous are listed.

References

Adeleke, Adedoyin. 2016. "Sustainability of Solar Mini-Grids in Nigeria." Working Paper. University of Ibadan & Centre for Petroleum, Energy Economic, and Law (CPEEL). www.academia.edu/30254688/SUSTAINABILITY_OF_SOLAR_MINI_GRIDS_IN_NIGERIA.

Agrawala, Shardul, Damien Dussaux, and Norbert Monti. 2020. "What Policies for Greening the Crisis Response and Economic Recovery? Lessons Learned from Past Green Stimulus Measures and Implications for the COVID-19 Crisis." Working Paper 164. OECD Environment Working Papers. Paris: OECD. https://doi.org/10.1787/c50f186f-en.

Agyeman, Julian. 2020. "Poor and Black 'Invisible Cyclists' Need to Be Part of Post-Pandemic Transport Planning Too." *The Conversation*. May 27. http://theconversation.com/poor-and-black-invisible cyclists-need-to-be-part-of-post-pandemic-transport-planning-too-139145.

Akinyele, Daniel, Juri Belikov, and Yoash Levron. 2018. "Challenges of Microgrids in Remote Communities: A STEEP Model Application." *Energies* 11 (2): 1–35.

Akinyele, Daniel, and Ramesh Kumar Rayudu. 2016. "Strategy for Developing Energy Systems for Remote Communities: Insights to Best Practices and Sustainability." *Sustainable Energy Technologies and Assessments* 16 (August): 106–27. https://doi.org/10.1016/j.seta.2016.05.001.

Alboiu, Vanessa, and Tony R. Walker. 2019. "Pollution, Management, and Mitigation of Idle and Orphaned Oil and Gas Wells in Alberta, Canada." *Environmental Monitoring and Assessment* 191 (10): 1–16. https://doi.org/10.1007/s10661-019-7780-x.

Allan, Bentley, Joanna I. Lewis, and Thomas Oatley. 2021. "Green Industrial Policy and the Global Transformation of Climate Politics." *Global Environmental Politics* 21 (4): 1–19. https://doi.org/10.1162/glep_a_00640.

Allan, Jennifer, Charles Donovan, Paul Ekins, et al. 2020. "A Net-Zero Emissions Economic Recovery from COVID-19." Working Paper 20–01. Oxford Smith School.

Alstone, Peter, Dimitry Gershenson, and Daniel M. Kammen. 2015. "Decentralized Energy Systems for Clean Electricity Access." *Nature Climate Change* 5 (4): 305–14. https://doi.org/10.1038/nclimate2512.

Anguiano, Dani. 2020. "California's Wildfire Hell: How 2020 Became the State's Worst Ever Fire Season." *The Guardian*. December 30.

www.theguardian.com/us-news/2020/dec/30/california-wildfires-north-complex-record.

Aoun, Gabriela. 2022. "California Wants Everyone to Drive EVs: How Will Low-Income People Afford Them?" *The Guardian*. October 13. www.theguardian.com/us-news/2022/oct/13/electric-vehicles-evs-california-low-income.

Appalachian Voices. 2022. "Advocates Praise Federal Guidance for Abandoned Mine Land Funding." May 24. https://appvoices.org/2022/05/24/aml-guid ance/.

Bakx, Kyle. 2020. "Indigenous Communities Secure $100M to Clean up Oil and Gas Wells." *CBC News*. November 27. www.cbc.ca/news/business/irc-savage-alberta-1.5818506.

Baldoni, Edoardo, Silvia Coderoni, Marco D'Orazio, Elisa Di Giuseppe, and Roberto Esposti. 2019. "The Role of Economic and Policy Variables in Energy-Efficient Retrofitting Assessment: A Stochastic Life Cycle Costing Methodology." *Energy Policy* 129 (June): 1207–19. https://doi.org/10.1016/j.enpol.2019.03.018.

Banister, David, Karen Anderton, David Bonilla, Moshe Givoni, and Tim Schwanen. 2011. "Transportation and the Environment." *Annual Review of Environment and Resources* 36 (1): 247–70. https://doi.org/10.1146/annurev-environ-032310-112100.

Bauer, Gordon, Chih-Wei Hsu, and Nic Lutsey. 2021. "When Might Lower-Income Drivers Benefit from Electric Vehicles? Quantifying the Economic Equity Implications of Electric Vehicle Adoption." Working Paper. International Council on Clean Transportation. https://theicct.org/wp-content/uploads/2021/06/EV-equity-feb2021.pdf.

Baurzhan, Saule, and Glenn P. Jenkins. 2016. "Off-Grid Solar PV: Is It an Affordable or Appropriate Solution for Rural Electrification in Sub-Saharan African Countries?" *Renewable and Sustainable Energy Reviews* 60 (July): 1405–18. https://doi.org/10.1016/j.rser.2016.03.016.

BBC News. 2021. "France Moves to Ban Short-Haul Domestic Flights." April 12. www.bbc.com/news/world-europe-56716708.

Bernstein, Aaron. 2020. "Coronavirus and Climate Change." *C-CHANGE: Harvard T.H. Chan School of Public Health* (blog). May 19. www.hsph.harvard.edu/c-change/subtopics/coronavirus-and-climate-change/.

Bhattacharyya, Subhes C. 2013. "Rural Electrification Experience from South-East Asia and South America." In Rural Electrification Through Decentralised Off-Grid Systems in Developing Countries, edited by Subhes Bhattacharyya, 157–84. London: Springer. https://doi.org/10.1007/978-1-4471-4673-5_7.

Bhattacharyya, Subhes C., and Debajit Palit. 2016. "Mini-Grid Based off-Grid Electrification to Enhance Electricity Access in Developing Countries: What Policies May Be Required?" *Energy Policy* 94 (July): 166–78. https://doi.org/10.1016/j.enpol.2016.04.010.

Biven, Megan. 2022. "Implementation of the Infrastructure Investment and Jobs Act (H.R. 3684): Title VI Methane Reduction Infrastructure Grant Program." Memo. True Transition. https://ohiorivervalleyinstitute.org/wp-content/uploads/2022/03/Memo-on-Methane-Reduction-Implementation-22-1.pdf.

Black, James. 2021. "Economic Impact of Scotland's Renewable Energy Sector." *FAI*. https://fraserofallander.org/publications/economic-impact-of-scotlands-renewable-energy-sector/.

Blimpo, Moussa P., and Malcolm Cosgrove-Davies. 2019. "Electricity Access in Sub-Saharan Africa." *AFD and World Bank*. https://openknowledge.worldbank.org/bitstream/handle/10986/31333/9781464813610.pdf?sequence=6&isAllowed=y.

Boemi, Sofia-Natalia, and Agis M. Papadopoulos. 2019. "Energy Poverty and Energy Efficiency Improvements: A Longitudinal Approach of the Hellenic Households." *Energy and Buildings* 197 (August): 242–50. https://doi.org/10.1016/j.enbuild.2019.05.027.

Boettner, Ted. 2021. *Repairing the Damage from Hazardous Abandoned Oil & Gas Wells*. Johnstown, Pennsylvania: Ohio River Valley Institute.

Bouchard, Catherine, Antonia Dibernardo, Jules Koffi, et al. 2019. "Increased Risk of Tick-Borne Diseases with Climate and Environmental Changes." *Canada Communicable Disease Report* 45 (4): 83–9. https://doi.org/10.14745/ccdr.v45i04a02.

Brand, Christian, Evi Dons, Esther Anaya-Boig, et al. 2021. "The Climate Change Mitigation Effects of Daily Active Travel in Cities." *Transportation Research Part D: Transport and Environment* 93 (April): 102764. https://doi.org/10.1016/j.trd.2021.102764.

Braubach, Matthias, and Arnaud Ferrand. 2013. "Energy Efficiency, Housing, Equity and Health." *International Journal of Public Health* 58 (3): 331–2. https://doi.org/10.1007/s00038-012-0441-2.

Bridge, Mikayla. 2022. "Innovative New Renewable Microgrid Bound for Far North QLD." *Energy Magazine*. March 8. www.energymagazine.com.au/innovative-new-renewable-microgrid-bound-for-far-north-qld/.

Brown, Katherine. 2021. "2020 Tied for Warmest Year on Record, NASA Analysis Shows." Text. NASA. January 14. www.nasa.gov/press-release/2020-tied-for-warmest-year-on-record-nasa-analysis-shows.

Brownlee, Michelle. 2013. "Financing Residential Energy Savings: Assessing Key Features of Residential Energy Retrofit Financing Programs."

Sustainable Prosperity. https://institute.smartprosperity.ca/sites/default/files/publications/files/Financing%20Residential%20Energy%20Savings.pdf.

Burch, Sarah, Aarti Gupta, Cristina Y. A. Inoue, et al. 2019. "New Directions in Earth System Governance Research." *Earth System Governance* 1 (January): 100006. https://doi.org/10.1016/j.esg.2019.100006.

C40, International Transport Workers' Federation. 2021. "The Future Is Public Transport." London. www.c40knowledgehub.org/s/article/The-Future-is-Public-Transport?language=en_US.

Calder, Devon. 2020. "The Case for Deep Retrofits." *The Atmospheric Fund.* https://taf.ca/wp-content/uploads/2020/09/TAF-Business-Case-Deep-retrofits_2020.pdf.

California Air Resources Board. n.d. "Clean Cars 4 All." Accessed January 30, 2023a. ww2.arb.ca.gov/our-work/programs/clean-cars-4-all.

n.d. "Clean Vehicle Rebate Program." Accessed January 30, 2023b. ww2.arb.ca.gov/sites/default/files/movingca/cvrp.html.

Cameron, Alienor, Gregory Claeys, Catarina Midoes, and Simone Tagliapietra. 2020. "A Just Transition Fund: How the EU Budget Can Best Assist in the Necessary Transition from Fossil Fuels to Sustainable Energy." *European Parliament.* www.bruegel.org/2020/05/a-just-transition-fund-how-the-eu-budget-can-best-assist-in-the-necessary-transition-from-fossil-fuels-to-sustainable-energy/.

Caprotti, Federico. 2014. "Eco-urbanism and the Eco-city, or, Denying the Right to the City?" *Antipode* 46 (5): 1285–303.

Carbon Tracker. 2020. "Billion Dollar Orphans: Why Millions of Oil and Gas Wells Could Become Wards of the State." *Carbon Tracker Initiative.* October 1. https://carbontracker.org/reports/billion-dollar-orphans/.

Carroll, David. 2021. "Taylor Announces $30 Million Funding for Territory Infrastructure Initiatives." *Pv Magazine Australia.* May 7. www.pv-magazine-australia.com/2021/05/07/taylor-announces-30-million-funding-for-territory-infrastructure-initiatives/.

Castillo Sánchez, Marta. 2021. "Renewable Energy Communities to Boost the Energy Transition in the Mediterranean." *REVOLVE* (blog). June 18. https://revolve.media/renewable-energy-communities-to-boost-the-energy-transition-in-the-mediterranean/.

CBC Radio. 2020. "'If the Polluter Doesn't Pay to Clean It up, Taxpayers Will Have to': Alberta's Growing Oil Well Problem." *CBC.* March 6. www.cbc.ca/radio/sunday/the-sunday-edition-for-march-8-2020-1.5482636/if-the-polluter-doesn-t-pay-to-clean-it-up-taxpayers-will-have-to-alberta-s-growing-oil-well-problem-1.5486689.

Center for International Environmental Law. 2021. *Toxic Assets: Making Polluters Pay When Wells Run Dry and the Bill Comes Due*. Washington, DC: CIEL. www.ciel.org/wp-content/uploads/2021/04/Toxic-Assets-Report.pdf.

Chen, Chen, John Wang, Jeff Kwong, et al. 2022. "Association between Long-Term Exposure to Ambient Air Pollution and COVID-19 Severity: A Prospective Cohort Study." *Canadian Medical Association Journal* 194 (20): E693–700. https://doi.org/10.1503/cmaj.220068.

Chowdhury, Sarwat. 2021. "South Korea's Green New Deal in the Year of Transition." *UNDP*. February 8. www.undp.org/blog/south-koreas-green-new-deal-year-transition.

City of Medellín. 2020. "Línea Estratégica 4. Ecociudad." www.medellin.edu.co/wp-content/uploads/DocumentoFinal_PlanDesarrolloMedellin2020-2023_MedellinFuturo.pdf.

Clean Vehicle Assistance Program. n.d. "Who We Serve." Accessed January 30, 2023. https://cleanvehiclegrants.org/who-we-serve/.

Climate Change Committee. 2021. "Progress in Reducing Emissions: 2021 Report to Parliament." www.theccc.org.uk/wp-content/uploads/2021/06/Progress-in-reducing-emissions-2021-Report-to-Parliament.pdf.

Cohan, Peter. 2020. "How COVID-19 Crunch Compares to Spanish Flu, Great Depression." *Forbes*. April 6. www.forbes.com/sites/petercohan/2020/04/06/how-covid-19-crunch-compares-to-spanish-flu-great-depression/?sh=24111cfc1798.

Committee of Public Accounts. 2021. "Green Homes Grant Voucher Scheme." *UK House of Commons*. https://publications.parliament.uk/pa/cm5802/cmselect/cmpubacc/635/summary.html.

Corkal, Vanessa. 2021. "Federal Fossil Fuel Subsidies in Canada: COVID-19 Edition." *Global Subsidies Initiative*. www.iisd.org/system/files/2021-02/fossil-fuel-subsidies-canada-covid-19.pdf.

Cozzi, Laura, Daniel Wetzel, Gianluca Tonolo, and Jacob Hyppolite. 2022. "For the First Time in Decades, the Number of People without Access to Electricity Is Set to Increase in 2022: Analysis." *IEA*. November 3. www.iea.org/commentaries/for-the-first-time-in-decades-the-number-of-people-without-access-to-electricity-is-set-to-increase-in-2022.

Crear-Perry, Joia, and Michael McAfee. 2020. "To Protect Black Americans from the Worst Impacts of COVID-19, Release Comprehensive Racial Data." *Scientific American Blog Network*. https://blogs.scientificamerican.com/voices/to-protect-black-americans-from-the-worst-impacts-of-covid-19-release-comprehensive-racial-data/.

Davis, Eric. 2021. "Cleaning the New Jersey Commute: Electrifying Transport as a Step Toward Environmental Justice." *Climate-XChange* (blog). April 15. https://climate-xchange.org/2021/04/15/cleaning-the-new-jersey-commute-electrifying-transport-as-a-step-toward-environmental-justice/.

De Souza, Mike, and Julia Wong. 2020. "Big Oil Companies Eligible for Millions from Federal Coronavirus Bailout to Clean up Sites." *Global News*. December 17. https://globalnews.ca/news/7527074/big-oil-coronavirus-bailout/.

Department for Business, Energy & Industrial Strategy. 2021. "Over 50,000 Households to Get Warmer, Greener Homes in £562 Million Boost." *Gov. UK*. March 23. www.gov.uk/government/news/over-50000-households-to-get-warmer-greener-homes-in-562-million-boost.

2022. "Social Housing Decarbonisation Fund Wave 1: Successful Bids." February 7. www.gov.uk/government/publications/social-housing-decarbonisation-fund-wave-1-successful-bids.

Department of Environment, Land, Water and Planning. 2021a. "Victoria's Climate Change Strategy." https://nla.gov.au/nla.obj-2964663316.

2021b. "Victorian Renewable Energy Zones Development Plan Directions Paper." *Victoria Government*. www.energy.vic.gov.au/__data/assets/pdf_file/0016/512422/DELWP_REZ-Development-Plan-Directions-Paper_Feb23-updated.pdf.

2021c. "Renewable Energy Zones." *Text*. Victoria: Victoria State Government. June 23. www.energy.vic.gov.au/renewable-energy/renewable-energy-zones.

Department of Finance Canada. 2020. "Canada's COVID-19 Economic Response Plan: New Support to Protect Canadian Jobs." *Backgrounders*. April 17. www.canada.ca/en/department-finance/news/2020/04/canadas-covid-19-economic-response-plan-new-support-to-protect-canadian-jobs.html.

Department of the Interior. 2022a. "Bipartisan Infrastructure Law Sec. 40601 Orphaned Well Program FY 2022 State Initial Grant Guidance." www.doi.gov/sites/doi.gov/files/state-initial-grant-guidance-4-11-22.pdf.

2022b. "Guidance on the Bipartisan Infrastructure Law Abandoned Mine Land Grant Implementation."

2022c. "Interior Department, Federal Partners Announce Interagency Effort to Clean Up Legacy Pollution, Implement Infrastructure Law." January 18. www.doi.gov/pressreleases/interior-department-federal-partners-announce-interagency-effort-clean-legacy.

2022d. "Biden-Harris Administration Releases Draft Guidance, Invites Public Comment on Bipartisan Infrastructure Law Abandoned Mine Land Grant Program." May 23. www.doi.gov/pressreleases/biden-harris-administra tion-releases-draft-guidance-invites-public-comment-bipartisan.

DeShazo, J. R., and James Di Filippo. 2021. *An Agenda for Equity Centered Clean Transportation*. Los Angeles: UCLA Luskin Center for Innovation. https://innovation.luskin.ucla.edu/wp-content/uploads/2021/04/An-Agenda-for-Equity-Centered-Clean-Transportation.pdf.

Detrow, Scott. 2015. "Energy-Efficiency Efforts May Not Pay Off." *Scientific American*. June 24. www.scientificamerican.com/article/energy-effi ciency-efforts-may-not-pay-off/.

Dickson, Duane, Noemie Tilghman, Tom Bonny, Kate Hardin, and Anshu Mittal. 2020. "The Future of Work in Oil, Gas and Chemicals." *Deloitte Insights*. October 5. www2.deloitte.com/us/en/insights/industry/ oil-and-gas/future-of-work-oil-and-gas-chemicals.html.

Dijk, Meine Pieter van. 2015. "Measuring Eco Cities, Comparing European and Asian Experiences: Rotterdam versus Beijing." *Asia Europe Journal* 13 (1): 75–94. https://doi.org/10.1007/s10308-014-0405-7.

Dincer, Ibrahim. 2000. "Renewable Energy and Sustainable Development: A Crucial Review." *Renewable and Sustainable Energy Reviews* 4 (2): 157–75. https://doi.org/10.1016/S1364-0321(99)00011-8.

Dolšak, Nives, and Aseem Prakash. 2022. "Three Faces of Climate Justice." *Annual Review of Political Science* 25 (1): 283–301. https://doi.org/ 10.1146/annurev-polisci-051120-125514.

Dufour, Lucile, Joachim Roth, and Angela Picciariello. 2022. *In Search of a Triple Win*. Winnipeg: IISD. www.iisd.org/publications/report/covid-19-impacts-on-clean-energy-transition-inequality-poverty.

Dunn, Katherine. 2020. "Dutch Government Announces Climate Conditions for KLM Bailout, Rare in Other Government Bailouts." *Fortune*. June 26. https://fortune.com/2020/06/26/airline-bailouts-climate-conditions-cor onavirus/.

Duran, Asligul Serasu, and Feyza G. Sahinyazan. 2021. "An Analysis of Renewable Mini-Grid Projects for Rural Electrification." *Socio-Economic Planning Sciences* 77 (October): 100999. https://doi.org/ 10.1016/j.seps.2020.100999.

Duranton, Hélène. 2021. "Can the City Cycling Boom Survive the End of the Covid-19 Pandemic?" *The Conversation*. March 3. http://theconversation .com/can-the-city-cycling-boom-survive-the-end-of-the-covid-19-pan demic-155913.

Ecocity Builders and International Ecocity Framework & Standards. 2010. "What Is an Ecocity?" February 10. https://ecocitybuilders.org/what-is-an-ecocity/.

Economidou, Marina. 2018. "Energy Efficiency Upgrades in Multi-Owner Residential Buildings: Review of Governance and Legal Issues in 7 EU Member States." *JRC Publications Repository.* June 1. https://publica tions.jrc.ec.europa.eu/repository/handle/JRC110289.

Edenhofer, Ottmar, Ramón Pichs-Madruga, Youba Sokona, et al., eds. 2011. *Renewable Energy Sources and Climate Change Mitigation: Special Report of the Intergovernmental Panel on Climate Change.* Cambridge: Cambridge University Press. https://doi.org/10.1017/CBO9781139 151153.

Ekpe, Unwana Macaulay, and Vincent Bassey Umoh. 2019. "Comparative Analysis of Electrical Power Utilization in Nigeria: From Conventional Grid to Renewable Energy-Based Mini-Grid Systems." *American Journal of Electrical Power and Energy Systems* 8 (5): 111–19. https://doi.org/10.11648/j.epes.20190805.12.

Emodi, Nnaemeka Vincent, and Nebedum Ekene Ebele. 2016. "Policies Enhancing Renewable Energy Development and Implications for Nigeria." *Sustainable Energy* 4 (1): 7–16. https://doi.org/10.12691/rse-4-1-2.

Energy and Mines Ministers' Conference and Natural Resources Canada. 2017. *Build Smart, Canada's Buildings Strategy: A Key Driver of the Pan-Canadian Framework on Clean Growth and Climate Change.* Energy and Mines Ministers' Conference, St. Andrews by-the-Sea, New Brunswick, August. http://publications.gc.ca/collections/collection_2018/rncan-nrcan/M4-150-2017-eng.pdf.

"Energy Policy Tracker." 2022. www.energypolicytracker.org/.

Energy Policy Tracker, Global Recovery Observatory, Greenness of Stimulus Index, and Green Recovery Tracker. 2021. "The Data Is in: Governments Must Green Their COVID-19 Recovery to Keep Global Temperature Rise to 1.5°C." International Institute for Sustainable Development. October 29. www.iisd.org/articles/covid-19-green-recovery-trackers-statement.

Ensing, Chris. 2021. "Ontario Government, Industry Group Want Feds to Fund Abandoned Well Clean Up." *CBC News.* September 3. www.cbc.ca/news/canada/windsor/industry-feds-wells-ontario-1.6162860.

Environmental Defense Fund. 2021. "New Jersey Becomes the Nation's Latest Clean Trucks State, Dumping Dirty Diesel." December 20. www.edf.org/media/new-jersey-becomes-nations-latest-clean-trucks-state-dumping-dirty-diesel.

n.d. "Advanced Clean Trucks Rule Is New Jersey's Road to Clean Transportation." Accessed January 30, 2023. www.edf.org/sites/default/files/documents/NewJerseyACTFactsheet.pdf.

European Commission. 2020a. "Just Transition Funding Sources." https://ec.europa.eu/info/strategy/priorities-2019-2024/european-green-deal/finance-and-green-deal/just-transition-mechanism/just-transition-funding-sources_en.

2020b. "Oil & Gas Transition Training Fund, Scotland." https://energy.ec.europa.cu/topics/oil-gas-and-coal/eu-coal-regions/resources/oil-gas-transition-training-fund-scotland_en.

2021. "State Aid: Commission Approves Aid in Battery Value Chain." January 26. https://ec.europa.eu/commission/presscorner/detail/en/ip_21_226.

n.d. "Energy Communities." Accessed June 6, 2022. https://energy.ec.europa.eu/topics/markets-and-consumers/energy-communities_en.

Evans, Bob. 2022. "Infrastructure Law's Grid Flexibility Program Has Opportunities for Smart Buildings." U.S. Green Building Council. March 28. www.usgbc.org/articles/infrastructure-law-s-grid-flexibility-program-has-opportunities-smart-buildings.

Evans, Geoff, and Liam Phelan. 2016. "Transition to a Post-Carbon Society: Linking Environmental Justice and Just Transition Discourses." *Energy Policy* 99 (December): 329–39. https://doi.org/10.1016/j.enpol.2016.05.003.

Federal Transit Administration. 2021. "Fact Sheet: All Stations Accessibility Program." www.transit.dot.gov/funding/grants/fact-sheet-all-stations-accessibility-program.

Fiorino, Daniel. 2017. *A Good Life on a Finite Earth: The Political Economy of Green Growth*. Oxford: Oxford University Press.

Fowlie, Meredith, Michael Greenstone, and Catherine Wolfram. 2015. "Are the Non-Monetary Costs of Energy Efficiency Investments Large? Understanding Low Take-Up of a Free Energy Efficiency Program." *American Economic Review* 105 (5): 201–4. https://doi.org/10.1257/aer.p20151011.

Frangoul, Anmar. 2021. "CO2 Emissions Set to Hit Record Levels in 2023 and There's 'no Clear Peak in Sight,' IEA Says." *CNBC*. July 20. www.cnbc.com/2021/07/20/co2-emissions-will-hit-record-levels-in-2023-iea-says.html.

Frappé-Sénéclauze, Tom-Pierre. 2021. "Federal Energy Efficiency Grant for Homeowners Falls Short on Funding, Program Design." Pembina Institute. May 27. www.pembina.org/media-release/federal-energy-efficiency-grant-homeowners-falls-short.

French, Kate. 2020. "Coal Mine Cleanup Works: A Look at the Potential Employment Needs for Mine Reclamation in the West." Western

Organization of Resource Councils. www.worc.org/media/Reclamation-Jobs-Report-FINAL_Nov-2020.pdf.

Fyfe, Caroline, Arthur Grimes, Shannon Minehan, and Pheobe Taptiklis. 2022. "Warmer Kiwis Study: Interim Report." Motu Working Paper 22–02. motu-www.motu.org.nz/wpapers/22_02.pdf

G7. 2021. "Carbis Bay G7 Summit Communique." The White House. June 13. www.whitehouse.gov/briefing-room/statements-releases/2021/06/13/carbis-bay-g7-summit-communique/.

Galgóczi, Béla. 2021. "From 'Just Transition' to the 'Eco-Social State'." In *The Palgrave Handbook of Environmental Labour Studies*, edited by Nora Räthzel, Dimitris Stevis, and David Uzzell, 539–62. Cham: Springer International. https://doi.org/10.1007/978-3-030-71909-8_23.

Garrett-Peltier, Heidi. 2017. "Green versus Brown: Comparing the Employment Impacts of Energy Efficiency, Renewable Energy, and Fossil Fuels Using an Input-Output Model." *Economic Modelling* 61 (February): 439–47. https://doi.org/10.1016/j.econmod.2016.11.012.

Gass, Philip. 2021. "Just Transition Measures for a Green Recovery." International Institute for Sustainable Development. May 21. www.iisd.org/articles/explainer/just-transition-measures-green-recovery.

Glatsky, Genevieve. 2021. "Medellín Strives to Become Latin America's First 'Eco-City'." *Aljazeera*. August 31. www.aljazeera.com/news/2021/8/31/medellin-strives-to-become-latin-americas-first-eco.

Global Alliance of Buildings and Construction. 2020. *2020 Global Status Report for Buildings and Construction*. UNEP: UN Environment Programme. https://globalabc.org/resources/publications/2020-global-status-report-buildings-and-construction.

Global Alliance of Buildings and Construction. 2021. *2021 Global Status Report for Buildings and Construction*. UNEP: UN Environment Programme. www.unep.org/resources/report/2021-global-status-report-buildings-and-construction.

Goldman Sachs. 2023. "The US Is Poised for an Energy Revolution." April 17. www.goldmansachs.com/intelligence/pages/the-us-is-poised-for-an-energy-revolution.html.

Government of Italy. 2021. "Piano Nazionale di Ripresa e Resilienza." www.governo.it/sites/governo.it/files/PNRR.pdf.

Government of Navarra. 2020. "El Gobierno de Navarra promueve una instalación fotovoltaica para el autoconsumo colectivo en el Navarra Arena." *Navarra.es*. October 7. www.navarra.es/es/noticias/2020/10/07/el-gobierno-de-navarra-promueve-una-instalacion-fotovoltaica-para-el-autoconsumo-colectivo-en-el-navarra-arena?pageBackId=363032&back=true.

Government of New Zealand. 2020a. "More Warmer Kiwi Homes." May 14. www.scoop.co.nz/stories/PA2005/S00124/more-warmer-kiwi-homes.htm.

2020b. "Green Light for Wellington and Wairarapa in $220m Nationwide Cycleways Package." *The Beehive*. August 20. www.beehive.govt.nz/release/green-light-wellington-and-wairarapa-220m-nationwide-cycle ways-package.

Government of Nigeria. 2020. "What You Need to Know About the Nigeria Economic Sustainability Plan: The Statehouse, Abuja." June 25. https://statehouse.gov.ng/news/what you-need-to-know-about-the-nigeria-eco nomic-sustainability-plan/.

Government of Nova Scotia. 2021. "Amendments to Electricity Act Create New Renewable Energy Opportunities." News Releases. April 7. https://novascotia.ca/news/release/?id=20210407004.

Government of Scotland. 2020a. "Supporting the Green Recovery." June 17. www.gov.scot/news/supporting-the-green-recovery/.

2020b. "Investing in Skills to Support Recovery." October 8. www.gov.scot/news/investing-in-skills-to-support-recovery/.

2021. "Sustainable Economic Recovery." June 16. www.gov.scot/news/sus tainable-economic-recovery/.

2022. "Transition Training Fund (TTF): FOI Release." March 2. www.gov .scot/publications/foi-202200277106/.

Government of Yukon. 2021. "Innovative and Renewable Energy Initiative Expanded to Support More Community Projects." July 27. https://yukon .ca/en/news/innovative-and-renewable-energy-initiative-expanded-sup port-more-community-projects.

Green, Fergus, and Noel Healy. 2022. "How Inequality Fuels Climate Change: The Climate Case for a Green New Deal." *One Earth* 5(6): 635–649. https://doi.org/10.1016/j.oneear.2022.05.005.

Green New Deal Group. 2008. "A Green New Deal." New Economics Foundation. https://neweconomics.org/uploads/files/8f737ea195 fe56db2f_xbm6ihwb1.pdf.

Greenpeace Europe. 2021. "European Airline Bailout Tracker." Greenpeace European Unit. June 9. www.greenpeace.org/eu-unit/issues/climate-energy/2725/airline-bailout-tracker.

Groom, Nichola. 2022. "U.S. to Spend $725 mln This Year on Abandoned Coal Mine Cleanup." *Reuters*. February 7, sec. United States. www.reuters .com/world/us/us-spend-725-mln-this-year-abandoned-coal-mine-cleanup-2022-02-07/.

Ground Water Protection Council. n.d. "Abandoned Mines." Accessed June 6, 2022. www.gwpc.org/topics/abandoned-mines/.

Gunn-Wright, Rhiana. 2020. "Policies and Principles of a Green New Deal." In *Winning the Green New Deal: Why We Must, How We Can*, edited by Varshini Prakash and Guido Girgenti, 67–93. New York: Simon and Schuster.

Gutiérrez, Aaron, Daniel Miravet, and Antoni Domènech. 2021. "COVID-19 and Urban Public Transport Services: Emerging Challenges and Research Agenda." *Cities & Health* 5 (sup1): S177–80. https://doi.org/10.1080/23748834.2020.1804291.

Haley, Brendan. 2020. "Energy Efficiency's Role in Canada's Economic Recovery." *Efficiency Canada* (blog). March 28. www.efficiencycanada.org/covid-19-part-2-energy-efficiencys-role-in-canadas-economic-recovery/.

Hansen, Ulrich Elmer, Mathilde Brix Pedersen, and Ivan Nygaard. 2015. "Review of Solar PV Policies, Interventions and Diffusion in East Africa." *Renewable and Sustainable Energy Reviews* 46 (June): 236–48. https://doi.org/10.1016/j.rser.2015.02.046.

Harvey, Fiona. 2020. "'Surprisingly Rapid' Rebound in Carbon Emissions Post-Lockdown." *The Guardian*. June 11, sec. Environment. www.theguardian.com/environment/2020/jun/11/carbon-emissions-in-surprisingly-rapid-surge-post-lockdown.

Hassan, Olumide, Stephen Morse, and Matthew Leach. 2020. "The Energy Lock-In Effect of Solar Home Systems: A Case Study in Rural Nigeria." *Energies* 13 (24): 6682. https://doi.org/10.3390/en13246682.

Henderson, Jason. 2020. "EVs Are Not the Answer: A Mobility Justice Critique of Electric Vehicle Transitions." *Annals of the American Association of Geographers* 110 (6): 1993–2010. https://doi.org/10.1080/24694452.2020.1744422.

Hepburn, Cameron, Brian O'Callaghan, Nicholas Stern, Joseph Stiglitz, and Dimitri Zenghelis. 2020. "Will COVID-19 Fiscal Recovery Packages Accelerate or Retard Progress on Climate Change?" *Oxford Review of Economic Policy* 36 (May): S359–S81. https://doi.org/10.1093/oxrep/graa015.

Hickel, Jason and Giorgos Kallis. 2020. "Is Green Growth Possible?" *New Political Economy* 25 (4): 469–86. https://doi.org/10.1080/13563467.2019.1598964.

Hinson, Suzanna, and Alex Adcock. 2021. "Green Homes Grant." Briefing Paper CBP 9235. House of Commons Library. https://researchbriefings.files.parliament.uk/documents/CBP-9235/CBP-9235.pdf.

Hoicka, Christina E., Paul Parker, and Jean Andrey. 2014. "Residential Energy Efficiency Retrofits: How Program Design Affects Participation and Outcomes." *Energy Policy* 65 (February): 594–607. https://doi.org/10.1016/j.enpol.2013.10.053.

Human Rights Watch. 2021. "Q&A on Fossil Fuel Subsidies." *Human Rights Watch* (blog). June 7. www.hrw.org/news/2021/06/07/qa-fossil-fuel-subsidies.

Hund, Kirsten, Daniele La Porta, Thao P. Fabregas, Tim Laing, and John Drexhage. 2020. "The Mineral Intensity of the Clean Energy Transition." World Bank. https://pubdocs.worldbank.org/en/961711588875536384/Minerals-for-Climate-Action-The-Mineral-Intensity-of-the-Clean-Energy-Transition.pdf.

IEA. 2020a. "Covid-19 and the Resilience of Renewables." www.iea.org/reports/renewables-2020/covid-19-and-the-resilience-of-renewables.

2020b. "Tracking Building Envelopes 2020." www.iea.org/reports/tracking-building-envelopes-2020.

2020c. "The Global Oil Industry Is Experiencing a Shock like No Other in Its History: Analysis." April 1. www.iea.org/articles/the-global-oil-industry-is-experiencing-shock-like-no-other-in-its-history.

2020d. "Changes in Transport Behaviour during the Covid-19 Crisis." May 27. www.iea.org/articles/changes-in-transport-behaviour-during-the-covid-19-crisis.

2020e. "Green Stimulus after the 2008 Crisis." June 29. www.iea.org/articles/green-stimulus-after-the-2008-crisis.

2020f. "Energy Technology Perspectives 2020." www.iea.org/reports/energy-technology-perspectives-2020

2020g. "Defining Energy Access: 2020 Methodology." October 13. www.iea.org/articles/defining-energy-access-2020-methodology.

2020h. "Projected Costs of Generating Electricity 2020." December. www.iea.org/reports/projected-costs-of-generating-electricity-2020.

2021a. "Coal 2021." https://iea.blob.core.windows.net/assets/f1d724d4-a753-4336-9f6e-64679fa23bbf/Coal2021.pdf.

2021b. "Global EV Outlook 2021." www.iea.org/reports/global-ev-outlook-2021.

2021c. "Oil 2021." www.iea.org/reports/oil-2021.

2021d. "Tracking Buildings 2021." www.iea.org/reports/tracking-buildings-2021.

2021e. "Transport." www.iea.org/topics/transport.

2021f. "Global Energy-Related CO2 Emissions by Sector." March 25. www.iea.org/data-and-statistics/charts/global-energy-related-co2-emissions-by-sector.

2021g. "Net Zero by 2050: A Roadmap for the Global Energy Sector." www.iea.org/reports/net-zero-by-2050.

2021h. "Korean New Deal: Digital New Deal, Green New Deal and Stronger Safety Net." July 16. www.iea.org/policies/11514-korean-new-deal-digital-new-deal-green-new-deal-and-stronger-safety-net.

2022a. "Gas Market Report, Q3-2022." https://iea.blob.core.windows.net/assets/c7e74868-30fd-440c-a616-488215894356/GasMarketReport%2CQ3-2022.pdf.

2022b. "Global Electric Vehicle Outlook 2022." https://iea.blob.core.windows.net/assets/ad8fb04c-4f75-42fc-973a-6e54c8a4449a/GlobalElectricVehicleOutlook2022.pdf.

2022c. "Renewable Energy Market Update 2022." https://iea.blob.core.windows.net/assets/d6a7300d-7919-4136-b73a-3541c33f8bd7/RenewableEnergyMarketUpdate2022.pdf.

2023. "Global EV Outlook 2023: Catching up with Climate Ambitions." Paris: IEA. www.iea.org/reports/global-ev-outlook-2023.

InfraCo Africa. 2021. "Investing to Scale up Multi-Sector Off-Grid Solutions." July 6. https://infracoafrica.com/investing-to-scale-up-multi-sector-off-grid-solutions/.

Initiative for Energy Justice. 2019. "Section 1: Defining Energy Justice: Connections to Environmental Justice, Climate Justice, and the Just Transition." *Initiative for Energy Justice* (blog). December 23. https://iejusa.org/section-1-defining-energy-justice/.

Insulate Britain. n.d. "Insulate Britain." Accessed June 6, 2022. www.insulatebritain.com.

International Civil Aviation Organization. 2022. "Effects of Novel Coronavirus (COVID-19) on Civil Aviation: Economic Impact Analysis." *Montreal*. www.icao.int/sustainability/Documents/Covid-19/ICAO_coronavirus_Econ_Impact.pdf.

International Labour Organization. 2015. *Guidelines for a Just Transition towards Environmentally Sustainable Economies and Societies for All.* Geneva: ILO. www.ilo.org/wcmsp5/groups/public/–ed_emp/–emp_ent/documents/publication/wcms_432859.pdf.

2020. "COVID-19 and the World of Work: Jump-Starting a Green Recovery with More and Better Jobs, Healthy and Resilient Societies." Report. ILO.

2021. "COVID-19 and the World of Work: Seventh Edition Updated Estimates and Analysis." www.ilo.org/wcmsp5/groups/public/—dgreports/—dcomm/documents/briefingnote/wcms_767028.pdf.

2022. "ILO Monitor on the World of Work." 9th ed. www.ilo.org/wcmsp5/groups/public/—dgreports/—dcomm/—publ/documents/publication/wcms_845642.pdf.

IPCC. 2014. "Climate Change 2014: Mitigation of Climate Change. Contribution of Working Group II to the Fifth Assessment Report of the Intergovernmental Panel on Climate Change." www.ipcc.ch/site/assets/uploads/2018/02/ipcc_wg3_ar5_chapter8.pdf.

80

References

2022. "Climate Change 2022: Mitigation of Climate Change (Working Group III Contribution to the Sixth Assessment Report)." www.ipcc.ch/report/ar6/wg3/.

IRENA. 2020. "Global Renewables Outlook: Energy Transformation 2050." Abu Dhabi: International Renewable Energy Agency. www.irena.org/-/media/Files/IRENA/Agency/Publication/2020/Apr/IRENA_GRO_Summary_2020.pdf.

2021a. "Tracking SDG7." https://trackingsdg7.esmap.org/data/files/down load-documents/2021_tracking_sdg7_executive_summary.pdf.

2021b. "Renewable Power Generation Costs in 2020." www.irena.org/publi cations/2021/Jun/Renewable-Power-Costs-in-2020.

Jeffords, Shawn. 2021. "Calls Grow for Action on Ontario's Thousands of Abandoned Oil and Gas Wells." *Global News*. June 13. https://globalnews .ca/news/7945982/calls-for-action-ontario-abandoned-oil-gas-wells/.

Jenkins, Kirsten, Darren McCauley, Raphael Heffron, Hannes Stephan, and Robert Rehner. 2016. "Energy Justice: A Conceptual Review." *Energy Research & Social Science* 11 (January): 174–82. https://doi.org/10.1016/j.erss.2015.10.004.

Johnson, Oliver, Zoha Shawoo, Sara Talebian, Eric Kemp-Benedict, and Andrea Lindblom. 2020. "Shaping a Sustainable and Low-Carbon Recovery That Spurs Industry Transition." *Leadership Group for Industry Transition*. www.sei.org/wp-content/uploads/2020/05/200508-green-recovery-short-brief-final.pdf22.pdf.

Josephs, Leslie. 2021. "Global Airline Industry Is Expected to Cut Losses in 2022 by 78% to $12 Billion in Slow Pandemic Recovery." *CNBC*. October 4. www.cnbc.com/2021/10/04/airlines-covid-recovery-2022-losses-to-fall.html.

Joss, Simon, Robert Cowley, and Daniel Tomozeiu. 2013. "Towards the 'Ubiquitous Eco-City': An Analysis of the Internationalisation of Eco-City Policy and Practice." *Urban Research & Practice* 6 (1): 54–74. https://doi.org/10.1080/17535069.2012.762216.

Just Transition Fund. n.d. "Abandoned Mine Land Fund." Accessed June 6, 2022. www.justtransitionfund.org/blueprint-policy/abandoned-mine-land-fund.

Just Transition Initiative. 2021. "A Just Green Recovery from COVID-19." Center for Strategic and International Studies (CSIS) and Climate Investment Funds (CIF). https://justtransitioninitiative.org/wp-content/uploads/2021/05/210526_JustGreenRecovery_-Covid19_Update.pdf.

Kagimu, Victor, and Taha Selim Ustun. 2016. "Novel Business Models and Policy Directions Based on SE4ALL Global Framework for Minigrids."

In *2016 IEEE International Conference on Emerging Technologies and Innovative Business Practices for the Transformation of Societies (EmergiTech)*, 251–56. https://doi.org/10.1109/EmergiTech.2016.7737348.

Kang, Mary, Adam R. Brandt, Zhong Zheng, et al. 2021. "Orphaned Oil and Gas Well Stimulus: Maximizing Economic and Environmental Benefits." *Elementa: Science of the Anthropocene* 9 (1): 1–13. https://doi.org/10.1525/elementa.2020.20.00161.

Kantamneni, Abhilash, and Brendan Haley. 2022. "Efficiency for All: A Review of Provincial/Territorial Low-Income Energy Efficiency Programs with Lessons for Federal Policy." *Efficiency Canada*. www.efficiencycanada.org/wp-content/uploads/2022/03/Low-Income-Energy-Efficiency-Programs-Final-Report-REVISED-with-COVER.pdf.

Kenner, Dario. 2019. *Carbon Inequality: The Role of the Richest in Climate Change*. London: Routledge. www.routledge.com/Carbon-Inequality-The-Role-of-the-Richest-in-Climate-Change/Kenner/p/book/9780367727666.

Khennas, Smail. 2012. "Understanding the Political Economy and Key Drivers of Energy Access in Addressing National Energy Access Priorities and Policies: African Perspective." *Energy Policy, Universal access to energy: Getting the framework right*, 47 (June): 21–26. https://doi.org/10.1016/j.enpol.2012.04.003.

Kimutai, Joyce, Clair Barnes, Mariam Zachariah et al. 2023. *Human-Induced Climate Change Increased Drought Severity in Horn of Africa*. London: Grantham Institute. https://spiral.imperial.ac.uk/bitstream/10044/1/103482/16/Scientific%20report-East_Africa_Drought_Final.pdf.

Koehl, Arnaud. 2021. "Urban Transport and COVID-19: Challenges and Prospects in Low- and Middle-Income Countries." *Cities & Health* 5 (sup1): S185–90. https://doi.org/10.1080/23748834.2020.1791410.

Kose, M. Ayhan, Peter Nagle, Franziska Ohnsorge, and Naotaka Sugawara. 2021. "What Has Been the Impact of COVID-19 on Debt? Turning a Wave into a Tsunami." Working Paper. Washington, DC: World Bank. https://doi.org/10.1596/1813-9450-9871.

Kretzmann, Hollin, Jennifer Koney, Katie Huffling et al. 2022. "Comments on State Orphan Well Grants Draft Guidance," March 30. www.biologicaldiversity.org/programs/climate_law_institute/pdfs/2022-03-30_Orphan_Well_Letter_to_Dept._of_Interior.pdf.

Ku, Arthur L., and John D. Graham. 2022. "Is California's Electric Vehicle Rebate Regressive? A Distributional Analysis." *Journal of Benefit-Cost Analysis* 13 (1): 1–19. https://doi.org/10.1017/bca.2022.2.

Kushler, Martin. 2015. "Residential Energy Efficiency Works: Don't Make a Mountain out of the." *ACEEE* (blog). June 25. www.aceee.org/blog/2015/06/residential-energy-efficiency-works.

Laborde Debucquet, David, Will Martin, and Rob Vos. 2020. "Poverty and Food Insecurity Could Grow Dramatically as COVID-19 Spreads." International Food Policy Research Institute (IFPRI) https://doi.org/10.2499/p15738coll2.133762_02.

Lawson, Alex. 2022. "Government Plans £6bn to Insulate UK Houses and Gives Go-Ahead for Sizewell C." *The Guardian*. November 17, sec. UK news. www.theguardian.com/uk-news/2022/nov/17/6bn-insulate-houses-sizewell-c-jeremy-hunt-energy-efficiency-autumn-statement.

Le Quéré, Corinne, Robert B. Jackson, Matthew W. Jones, et al. 2020. "Temporary Reduction in Daily Global CO2 Emissions during the COVID-19 Forced Confinement." *Nature Climate Change* 10 (7): 647–53. https://doi.org/10.1038/s41558-020-0797-x.

Lee, Marc, Eugene Kung, and Jason Owen. 2011. "Fighting Energy Poverty in the Transition to Zero-Emission Housing: A Framework for BC." Canadian Centre for Policy Alternatives. http://epe.lac-bac.gc.ca/100/200/300/cdn_centre_policy_alternatives/2011/Fighting-Energy-Poverty.pdf.

Lewis, Joanna I. 2021. "Green Industrial Policy After Paris: Renewable Energy Policy Measures and Climate Goals." *Global Environmental Politics* 21 (4): 42–63. https://doi.org/10.1162/glep_a_00636.

Liang, Jing, Yueming (Lucy) Qiu, Pengfei Liu, Pan He, and Denise L. Mauzerall. 2023. "Effects of Expanding Electric Vehicle Charging Stations in California on the Housing Market." *Nature Sustainability*, January, 1–10. https://doi.org/10.1038/s41893-022-01058-5.

Linn, Joshua. 2022. "Balancing Equity and Effectiveness for Electric Vehicle Subsidies." Working Paper. Resources for the Future. https://media.rff.org/documents/WP_22-7_January_2022.pdf.

Lovaas, Deron. 2022. "Transportation in the Bipartisan Infrastructure Law: Are We There Yet?" NDRC. *Expert Blog* (blog). November 18. www.nrdc.org/bio/deron-lovaas/transportation-bipartisan-infrastructure-law-are-we-there-yet.

Mack, Eric. 2021. "'Extraordinary Rainfall' Drops Year's Worth In Just 3 Days On China's IPhone City." *Forbes*, July 21. www.forbes.com/sites/ericmack/2021/07/21/extraordinary-rainfall-drops-years-worth-in-just-3-days-on-chinas-iphone-city/?sh=28f128e29f76.

Mahapatra, Sadhan, and Srinivasaiah Dasappa. 2012. "Rural Electrification: Optimising the Choice between Decentralised Renewable Energy Sources and Grid Extension." *Energy for Sustainable Development* 16 (2): 146–54. https://doi.org/10.1016/j.esd.2012.01.006.

Maharashtra Energy Development Agency. 2021. "Policies." www.mahaurja .com/meda/en/policies.

Martin, Adrian, Maria Teresa Armijos, Brendan Coolsaet, et al. 2020. "Environmental Justice and Transformations to Sustainability." *Environment: Science and Policy for Sustainable Development* 62 (6): 19–30. https://doi.org/10.1080/00139157.2020.1820294.

McCauley, Darren, Raphael Heffron, Hannes Stephan, and Kirsten Jenkins. 2013. "Advancing Energy Justice: The Triumvirate of Tenets." *International Energy Law Review* 32 (3): 107–10.

McCullough, Sarah R., Adonia Lugo, and Rebecca van Stokkum. 2019. "Making Bicycling Equitable: Lessons from Sociocultural Research." White Paper. Institute of Transportation Studies. https://escholarship.org/ uc/item/37s8b56q.

McKinsey & Company. 2022. "COVID-19's Impact on the Global Aviation Sector." March 31. www.mckinsey.com/industries/travel-logistics-and-infrastructure/our-insights/taking-stock-of-the-pandemics-impact-on-glo bal-aviation.

Meckling, Jonas. 2021. "Making Industrial Policy Work for Decarbonization." *Global Environmental Politics* 21 (4): 134–47. https://doi.org/10.1162/ glep_a_00624.

Meckling, Jonas, Nina Kelsey, Eric Biber, and John Zysman. 2015. "Winning Coalitions for Climate Policy." *Science* 349 (6253): 1170–1. https://doi .org/10.1126/science.aab1336.

Mernit, Judith. 2021. "The Oil Well Next Door: California's Silent Health Hazard." *Yale E360* (blog). March 31. https://e360.yale.edu/features/the-oil-well-next-door-californias-silent-health-hazard.

Meyer, Robinson. 2019. "A Centuries-Old Idea Could Revolutionize Climate Policy." *The Atlantic.* February 19. www.theatlantic.com/science/archive/ 2019/02/green-new-deal-economic-principles/582943/.

Ministry of Energy. 2018. "Kenya National Electrification Strategy." Government of Kenya. https://pubdocs.worldbank.org/en/413001554 284496731/Kenya-National-Electrification-Strategy-KNES-Key-Highlights-2018.pdf.

2021. "Energy Sector Commitments to Mitigate Against Climate Change." Government of Kenya.

Moerenhout, Tom. 2021. "Are We Ready for the Electric Vehicles Revolution?" *Columbia/SIPA Center on Global Energy Policy* (blog). December 15.

www.energypolicy.columbia.edu/research/interview/are-we-ready-elec tric-vehicles-revolution-qa-dr-tom-moerenhout.

Moloney, Anastasia. 2021. "Colombia's Medellín Plants 'Green Corridors' to Beat Rising Heat." *Reuters*. July 28. www.reuters.com/article/colombia-heatwave-environment-nature-idUSL8N2OY69Q.

Morton, Adam. 2020. "Scott Morrison's 'Gas-Led Recovery': What Is It and Will It Really Make Energy Cheaper?" *The Guardian*. September 16, sec. Environment. www.theguardian.com/environment/2020/sep/17/scott-morri sons-gas-led-recovery-what-is-it-and-will-it-really-make-energy-cheaper.

Mugisha, Joshua, Mike Ratemo, Bienvenu Keza, and Hayriye Kahveci. 2021. "Assessing the Opportunities and Challenges Facing the Development of Off-Grid Solar Systems in Eastern Africa: The Cases of Kenya, Ethiopia, and Rwanda." *Energy Policy* 150: 112131.

Mullen, Caroline, and Greg Marsden. 2016. "Mobility Justice in Low Carbon Energy Transitions." *Energy Research & Social Science* 18 (August): 109–17. https://doi.org/10.1016/j.erss.2016.03.026.

Mwirigi, Cosmas. 2020. "World Bank Offers $4.6 m Credit for off-Grid Solar Panels and Cook Stoves in Kenya." *Pv Magazine International*. October 27. www.pv-magazine.com/2020/10/27/world-bank-offers-4-6m-credit-for-off-grid-solar-panels-and-cook-stoves-in-kenya/.

Nahm, Jonas M., Scot M. Miller, and Johannes Urpelainen. 2022. "G20's US$14-Trillion Economic Stimulus Reneges on Emissions Pledges." *Nature* 603 (7899): 28–31. https://doi.org/10.1038/d41586-022-00540-6.

National Oceanic and Atmospheric Administration. 2021. "Record-Breaking Atlantic Hurricane Season Draws to an End." www.noaa.gov/media-release/record-breaking-atlantic-hurricane-season-draws-to-end.

Natural Resources Canada. 2021a. "Canada Invests in Cutting-Edge Indigenous Geothermal Electricity Production Facility." News Releases. March 12. www.canada.ca/en/natural-resources-canada/news/2021/03/canada-invests-in-cutting-edge-indigenous-geothermal-electricity-production-facility.html.

2021b. "Canada Greener Homes Grant." March 17. www.nrcan.gc.ca/energy-efficiency/homes/canada-greener-homes-grant/23441.

2022. "Clean Energy for Rural and Remote Communities Program." April 26. www.nrcan.gc.ca/reducingdiesel.

New Jersey Board of Public Utilities. 2021. "Multi-Unit Dwelling (MUD) Electric Vehicle Program." https://njcleanenergy.com/files/file/EV/MUD %20application%20final%201_24_22.pdf.

New Jersey Department of Community Affairs. 2021. "DCA Model Statewide Municipal EV Ordinance." www.nj.gov/dca/dlps/home/modelE Vordinance.shtml.

New Jersey Office of the Governor. 2021. "Governor Murphy Announces $100 Million Investment in Clean Transportation Projects." February 16. www .nj.gov/governor/news/news/562021/20210216a.shtml.

New York State. 2020. "Governor Cuomo Announces Clean Energy Investments to Benefit Over 350,000 Low-to-Moderate Income Households." *NYSERDA*. July 27. www.nyserda.ny.gov/About/Newsroom/2020-Announcements/ 2020-07-27-Governor-Cuomo-Announces-Clean-Energy-Investments-to-Benefit-Over-350000-Low-to-moderate-Income-Households.

2021. "Governor Cuomo Announces $52.5 Million Available for Community Solar Projects That Support Underserved New Yorkers." *NYSERDA*. July 20. www.nyserda.ny.gov/About/Newsroom/2021-Announcements/ 2021-07-20-Governor-Cuomo-Announces-52-5-Million-Available-for-Community-Solar-Projects-that-Support-Underserved-New-Yorkers.

Newell, Peter. 2022. "Climate Justice." *The Journal of Peasant Studies* 49 (5): 915–23. https://doi.org/10.1080/03066150.2022.2080062.

Nicol, Caroline, Ben Segel-Brown, and Salma Mohamed Ahmed. 2021. "Urban, Rural, and Northern Indigenous Housing." Parliamentary Budget Office. https://pbo-dpb.s3.ca-central-1.amazonaws.com/artefacts/ 5b2407108abe40544f4c66d4a7fe08c47aecce914911c2f7e3bbcad23a 2070fc.

Nkiriki, Joan, and Taha Selim Ustun. 2017. "Mini-Grid Policy Directions for Decentralized Smart Energy Models in Sub-Saharan Africa." In *2017 IEEE PES Innovative Smart Grid Technologies Conference Europe (ISGT-Europe)*, Turin, Italy: 1–6. https://doi.org/10.1109/ISGTEurope .2017.8260217.

Nwozor, Agaptus, Segun Oshewolo, Gbenga Owoeye, and Onjefu Okidu. 2021. "Nigeria's Quest for Alternative Clean Energy Development: A Cobweb of Opportunities, Pitfalls and Multiple Dilemmas." *Energy Policy* 149 (February): 112070. https://doi.org/10.1016/j.enpol.2020.112070.

O'Callaghan, Brian, and Em Murdock. 2021. "Are We Building Back Better? Evidence from 2020 and Pathways for Inclusive Green Recovery Spending." Global Recovery Observatory. www.unep.org/resources/publi cation/are-we-building-back-better-evidence-2020-and-pathways-inclu sive-green.

O'Callaghan, Brian, Nigel Yau, and Cameron Hepburn. 2022. "How Stimulating Is a Green Stimulus? The Economic Attributes of Green Fiscal Spending." *Annual Review of Environment and Resources* 47: 697–723.

Odin, Goddey. 2018. "Nigeria Ranked 2nd Largest Electricity Access Deficit in World as 80 m Homes Live without Power." March 28. www.businessaml ive.com/nigeria-ranked-2nd-largest-electricity-access-deficit-in-world-as-80 m-homes-live-without-power/.

OECD. 2020a. "Building Back Better: A Sustainable, Resilient Recovery after COVID-19." www.oecd.org/coronavirus/policy-responses/building-back-better-a-sustainable-resilient-recovery-after-covid-19-52b869f5/.

2020b. "Making the Green Recovery Work for Jobs, Income and Growth." https://oecd.org/coronavirus/policy-responses/making-the-green-recov ery-work-for-jobs-income-and-growth-a505f3e7/.

Ogbonnaya, Chukwuma, Chamil Abeykoon, Usman Damo, and Ali Turan. 2019. "The Current and Emerging Renewable Energy Technologies for Power Generation in Nigeria: A Review." *Thermal Science and Engineering Progress* 13 (October): 100390. https://doi.org/10.1016/j.tsep.2019.100390.

Parliamentary Budget Office. 2022. "Estimated Cost of Cleaning Canada's Orphan Oil and Gas Wells." https://distribution-a617274656661637473.pbo-dpb.ca/ 44de649e994977a9771ff83959ba6b9563f5c1352ec3ba4f83c4d256f40 a6b41.

Palmer, Ian. 2022. "How Scotland Is Juggling Oil and Gas and Jobs in Their Transition to Renewables." *Forbes*, May 25. www.forbes.com/sites/ianpal mer/2022/05/25/how-scotland-is-juggling-oil-and-gas-and-jobs-in-their-transition-to-renewables/?sh=2bdeecd03971

Peacock, Bella. 2021. "Queensland Approves $23 Million Renewable Energy Training Facility: Pv Magazine Australia." *Pv Magazine Australia*. July 28. www.pv-magazine-australia.com/2021/07/28/queensland-approves-23-million-renewable-energy-training-facility/.

Pembina Institute. 2020. "Diesel Reduction Progress in Remote Communities." www.pembina.org/reports/diesel-reduction-progress-research-summary-pdf.pdf.

Persram, Sonja. 2011. "Property Assessed Payments for Energy Retrofits and Other Financing Options." David Suzuki Foundation. https://davidsuzuki .org/science-learning-centre-article/property-assessed-payments-energy-retrofits-financing-options/.

Pettifor, Ann. 2019. *The Case for the Green New Deal*. Brooklyn: Verso Books.

Phillips, Nicky. 2020. "Climate Change Made Australia's Devastating Fire Season 30% More Likely." *Nature*. March. https://doi.org/10.1038/ d41586-020-00627-y.

Plumer, Brad. 2015. "Energy Efficiency Can Be Incredibly Valuable: But We Do Need to Measure It Properly." *Vox*. June 26. www.vox.com/2015/6/26/ 8849695/weatherization-e2e-study-response.

Pollin, Robert, and Shouvik Chakraborty. 2020. "Job Creation Estimates Through Proposed Economic Stimulus Measures." *PERI*. https://peri.umass.edu/ images/Pollin–Sierra_Club_Job_Creation–9–9–20–FINALpdf.

Pollin, Robert, Heidi Garrett-Peltier, James Heintz, and Bracken Hendricks. 2014. "Green Growth: A U.S. Program for Controlling Climate Change and Expanding Job Opportunities." *PERI*. https://peri.umass.edu/publica tion/item/585-green-growth-a-u-s-program-for-controlling-climate-change-and-expanding-job-opportunities.

Queensland Treasury. 2021. "Queensland Renewable Energy and Hydrogen Jobs Fund." June 10. www.treasury.qld.gov.au/programs-and-policies/ queensland-renewable-energy-and-hydrogen-jobs-fund/.

Raimi, Daniel, Neelesh Nerurkar, and Jason Bordoff. 2020. "Green Stimulus for Oil and Gas Workers: Considering a Major Federal Effort to Plug Orphaned and Abandoned Wells." Columbia Center on Global Energy Policy. www.energypolicy.columbia.edu/sites/default/files/file-uploads/ OrphanWells_CGEP-Report_071620.pdf.

Raitbaur, Louisa. 2021. "The New German Coal Laws: A Difficult Balancing Act." *Climate Law* 11 (2): 176–94. https://doi.org/10.1163/18786561-11020003.

Riofrancos, Thea, Alissa Kendall, Kristi Dayemo, et al. 2023. "Achieving Zero Emissions with More Mobility and Less Mining." Climate + Community Project. www.climateandcommunity.org/_files/ugd/d6378b_3b79520 a747948618034a2b19b9481a0.pdf.

Rodrik, Dani. 2014. "Green Industrial Policy." *Oxford Review of Economic Policy* 30 (3): 469–91.

Rowlatt, Justin. 2020. "Could the Coronavirus Crisis Finally Finish off Coal?" *BBC News*. June 9. www.bbc.com/news/science-environment-52968716.

Russo, Rémi, and Virginie Boutueil. 2011. "Toward Low Carbon Mobility : Tackling Road Transport Emissions." Working Paper. www.researchgate .net/publication/241759076_Toward_low_carbon_mobility_Tackling_ road_transport_emissions.

Ryan, Sadie J., Catherine A. Lippi, and Fernanda Zermoglio. 2020. "Shifting Transmission Risk for Malaria in Africa with Climate Change: A Framework for Planning and Intervention." *Malaria Journal* 19 (1): 170. https://doi.org/10.1186/s12936-020-03224-6.

Sadasivam, Naveena. 2022. "Abandoned Oil Well Counts Are Exploding: Now That There's Money on the Table." *Grist*. January 21. https://grist.org/ energy/abandoned-oil-wells-cleanup-infrastructure-law/.

Saha, Devashree. 2020. "Ensuring a Fair Transition for US Fossil Fuel Workers in Economic Recovery." World Resources Institute. May 19. www.wri.org/ insights/ensuring-fair-transition-us-fossil-fuel-workers-economic-recovery.

Sanchez, Lourdes, RIchard Bridle, Vanessa Corkal, et al. 2021. "Achieving a Fossil-Free Recovery." *IISD*. www.iisd.org/publications/achieving-fos sil-free-recovery.

Santos Ayllón, Lara M., and Kirsten E. H. Jenkins. 2023. "Energy Justice, Just Transitions and Scottish Energy Policy: A Re-Grounding of Theory in Policy Practice." *Energy Research & Social Science* 96 (February): 102922. https://doi.org/10.1016/j.erss.2022.102922.

Schlosberg, David. 2013. "Theorising Environmental Justice: The Expanding Sphere of a Discourse." *Environmental Politics* 22 (1): 37–55. https://doi .org/10.1080/09644016.2013.755387.

Schlosberg, David, and Lisette B. Collins. 2014. "From Environmental to Climate Justice: Climate Change and the Discourse of Environmental Justice." *WIREs Climate Change* 5 (3): 359–74. https://doi.org/10.1002/wcc.275.

Seetharaman, Krishna Moorthy, Nitin Patwa, Saravanan, and Yash Gupta. 2019. "Breaking Barriers in Deployment of Renewable Energy." *Heliyon* 5 (1): e01166. https://doi.org/10.1016/j.heliyon.2019.e01166.

SEforALL. 2020. "The Recover Better with Sustainable Energy Guide for African Countries." www.seforall.org/system/files/2020-08/RB-Africa-SEforALL.pdf.

2021. "Project: Achieving Economies of Scale in the Nigerian Solar Value Chain." www.seforall.org/policy-and-regulatory-frameworks/project-nigerian-solar-value-chain.

Senate Democrats. 2022. "Summary: The Inflation Reduction Act of 2022." www.democrats.senate.gov/imo/media/doc/inflation_reduction_act_one_ page_summary.pdf.

Seymour, Ann M. 2020. "Canada's Unequal Health System May Make Remote Indigenous Communities More Vulnerable to the Coronavirus." *The Conversation*. April 22. http://theconversation.com/canadas-unequal-health-system-may-make-remote-indigenous-communities-more-vulner able-to-the-coronavirus-134963.

Sharpe, Ben, and Gordon Bauer. 2021. "Low-Income Households Could Benefit Most from EVs, but Policy Fixes Are Needed." *Electric Autonomy Canada*. April 13. https://electricautonomy.ca/2021/04/13/ev-equity-incentive-policies/.

Shilling, Fraser, Tricia Nguyen, Malak Saleh, et al. 2021. "A Reprieve from US Wildlife Mortality on Roads during the COVID-19 Pandemic." *Biological Conservation* 256 (April): 109013. https://doi.org/10.1016/j.biocon .2021.109013.

Siciliano, Giuseppina, Linda Wallbott, Frauke Urban, Anh Nguyen Dang, and Markus Lederer. 2021. "Low-Carbon Energy, Sustainable Development, and Justice: Towards a Just Energy Transition for the Society and the

Environment." *Sustainable Development* 29: 1049–1061. https://doi.org/10.1002/sd.2193.

Skills Development Scotland. 2021. "£14 m Programme Targets New Jobs and Economic Recovery in Aberdeen and Aberdeenshire." October 14. www.skillsdevelopmentscotland.co.uk/news-events/2021/october/14 m-programme-targets-new-jobs-and-economic-recovery-in-aberdeen-and-aberdeenshire/.

Speers-Roesch, Alex. 2020. "Oil Industry Leveraging Pandemic to Pressure Government for Climate-Wrecking Favours in Newfoundland Offshore." *Greenpeace Canada* (blog). August 19. www.greenpeace.org/canada/en/story/41378/oil-industry-leveraging-pandemic-to-pressure-government-for-climate-wrecking-favours-in-newfoundland-offshore/.

Stanford, Jim. 2021. "Employment Transitions and the Phase-Out of Fossil Fuels." *The Centre for Future Work.* https://centreforfuturework.ca/wp-content/uploads/2021/01/Employment-Transitions-Report-Final.pdf.

State of California. 2021. "Governor Newsom Signs Climate Action Bills, Outlines Historic $15 Billion Package to Tackle the Climate Crisis and Protect Vulnerable Communities." California Governor. September 23. www.gov.ca.gov/2021/09/23/governor-newsom-signs-climate-action-bills-outlines-historic-15-billion-package-to-tackle-the-climate-crisis-and-protect-vulnerable-communities/.

Stevis, Dimitris. 2023. *Just Transitions: Promise and Contestations.* Elements in Earth System Governance. Cambridge: Cambridge University Press.

Stevis, Dimitris, and Romain Felli. 2015. "Global Labour Unions and Just Transition to a Green Economy." *International Environmental Agreements: Politics, Law and Economics* 15 (1): 29–43. https://doi.org/10.1007/s10784-014-9266-1.

Stevis, Dimitris, Edouard Morena, and Dunja Krause. 2019. "Introduction: The Genealogy and Contemporary Politics of Just Transitions." In *Just Transitions*, edited by Edouard Morena, Dunja Krause, and Dimitris Stevis, 1–31. London: Pluto Press.

Sustainable Buildings Canada. 2021. "Deep Energy Retrofit Energy Modelling Guide." https://sbcanada.org/wp-content/uploads/2017/04/Deep-Energy-Retrofits-Guide-V1.pdf.

Táíwò, Olúfẹ́mi, and Beba Cibralic. 2020. "The Case for Climate Reparations." *Foreign Policy.* October 10. https://foreignpolicy.com/2020/10/10/case-for-climate-reparations-crisis-migration-refugees-inequality/.

Takouleu, Jean Marie. 2021. "KENYA: InfraCo Africa and RVE.SOL Join Forces for 22 Solar Mini-Grids in Busia County." *Afrik 21* (blog). July 7.

www.afrik21.africa/en/kenya-infraco-africa-and-rve-sol-join-forces-for-22-solar-mini-grids-in-busia-county/.

Tarekegne, Bethel. 2020. "Just Electrification: Imagining the Justice Dimensions of Energy Access and Addressing Energy Poverty." *Energy Research & Social Science* 70 (December): 101639. https://doi.org/10.1016/j.erss.2020.101639.

Taylor, Kira. 2020. "EU Agrees to Set aside 37% of Recovery Fund for Green Transition." *Euractiv.* December 18. www.euractiv.com/section/energy-environment/news/eu-agrees-to-set-aside-37-of-recovery-fund-for-green-transition/.

Tienhaara, Kyla. 2018. *Green Keynesianism and the Global Financial Crisis.* London: Routledge.

Tienhaara, Kyla, and Joanna Robinson, eds. 2022. *Routledge Handbook on the Green New Deal.* London: Routledge.

Tigue, Kristoffer. 2022. "As States Move to Electrify Their Fleets, Activists Demand Greater Environmental Justice Focus." *Inside Climate News.* January 24. https://insideclimatenews.org/news/24012022/electric-vehicles-environmental-justice/.

Timperley, Jocelyn. 2021. "The Broken $100-Billion Promise of Climate Finance: And How to Fix It." *Nature.* October 20. www.nature.com/articles/d41586-021-02846-3.

TNN Agency. 2020. "GO Issued Promising 9-Hr Power to Farmers, Solar Energy to Be Tapped: ET EnergyWorld." *ETEnergyworld.Com.* June 16. https://energy.economictimes.indiatimes.com/news/renewable/go-issued-promising-9-hr-power-to-farmers-solar-energy-to-be-tapped/76397415.

Tollefson, Jeff. 2020. "Why Deforestation and Extinctions Make Pandemics More Likely." *Nature* 584 (7820): 175–6. https://doi.org/10.1038/d41586-020-02341-1.

2021. "COVID Curbed Carbon Emissions in 2020: But Not by Much." *Nature* 589 (7842): 343. https://doi.org/10.1038/d41586-021-00090-3.

Tonn, Bruce Edward, David Carroll, Erin M. Rose, et al. 2015. "Weatherization Works II: Summary of Findings from the ARRA Period Evaluation of the U.S. Department of Energy's Weatherization Assistance Program." https://doi.org/10.2172/1223654.

Transport Canada. 2021. "New Measures to Support Essential Air Access to Remote Communities." July 7. www.canada.ca/en/transport-canada/news/2020/08/new-measures-to-support-essential-air-access-to-remote-communities.html.

UNEP. 2009. "A Global Green New Deal." Policy Brief. https://wedocs.unep.org/bitstream/handle/20.500.11822/7903/A_Global_Green_New_Deal_Policy_Brief.pdf?sequence=3&%3BisAllowed=.

2019. "Emissions Gap Report 2019." UNEP: UN Environment Programme. www.unep.org/resources/emissions-gap-report-2019.

2021. "Are We Building Back Better? Evidence from 2020 and Pathways for Inclusive Green Recovery Spending." Nairobi: UNEP. www.unep.org/resources/publication/are-we-building-back-better-evidence-2020-and-pathways-inclusive-green.

UNFCCC Secretariat. 2020. "Just Transition of the Workforce, and the Creation of Decent Work and Quality Jobs." *UNFCCC*. https://unfccc.int/sites/default/files/resource/Just%20transition.pdf.

US Department of Energy. 2022. "Inflation Reduction Act Summary." www.energy.gov/sites/default/files/2022-10/IRA-Energy-Summary_web.pdf.

US Department of Transportation. 2022. "Fact Sheet: Equity in the Bipartisan Infrastructure Law." www.transportation.gov/bipartisan-infrastructure-law/fact-sheet-equity-bipartisan-infrastructure-law.

US EPA. n.d. "Routes to Lower Greenhouse Gas Emissions Transportation Future." Accessed June 9, 2022. www.epa.gov/greenvehicles/routes-lower-greenhouse-gas-emissions-transportation-future.

van Bommel, Natascha and Johanna I. Höffken. 2021. "Energy Justice within, between and beyond European Community Energy Initiatives: A Review." *Energy Research & Social Science* 79: 102157. https://doi.org/10.1016/j.erss.2021.102157.

Van Veelen, Bregje. 2018. "Negotiating Energy Democracy in Practice: Governance Processes in Community Energy Projects." *Environmental Politics* 27 (4): 644–65. https://doi.org/10.1080/09644016.2018.1427824.

Venter, Zander, Kristin Aunan, Sourangsu Chowdhury, and Jos Lelieveld. 2020. "COVID-19 Lockdowns Cause Global Air Pollution Declines." *PNAS* 117 (32): 18984–90. https://doi.org/10.1073/pnas.2006853117.

Vickerman, Roger. 2021. "Will Covid-19 Put the Public Back in Public Transport? A UK Perspective." *Transport Policy* 103 (March): 95–102. https://doi.org/10.1016/j.tranpol.2021.01.005.

Wei, Max, Shana Patadia, and Daniel M. Kammen. 2010. "Putting Renewables and Energy Efficiency to Work: How Many Jobs Can the Clean Energy Industry Generate in the US?" *Energy Policy* 38 (2): 919–31. https://doi.org/10.1016/j.enpol.2009.10.044.

Welker, Lukas, Joachim Roth, and Ivetta Gerasimchuk. 2022. "2020–21 Global Recovery Analysis." *Energy Policy Tracker*. www.energypolicytracker.org/2020-21-global-recovery-analysis/.

Whitehouse, Simon. 2021. "Federal Home Retrofit Program Swamped by NWT Demand." *NNSL Media*. August 16. www.nnsl.com/news/federal-home-retrofit-program-swamped-by-nwt-demand-2/.

White-Newsome, Jalonne L., Phyllis Meadows, and Chris Kabel. 2018. "Bridging Climate, Health, and Equity: A Growing Imperative." *American Journal of Public Health* 108 (Suppl 2): S72–3. https://doi.org/10.2105/AJPH.2017.304133.

Williams, Nathaniel J., Paulina Jaramillo, Jay Taneja, and Taha Selim Ustun. 2015. "Enabling Private Sector Investment in Microgrid-Based Rural Electrification in Developing Countries: A Review." *Renewable and Sustainable Energy Reviews* 52 (December): 1268–81. https://doi.org/10.1016/j.rser.2015.07.153.

Woo, Andrea. 2021. "Nearly 600 People Died in B.C. Summer Heat Wave, Vast Majority Seniors: Coroner." *The Globe and Mail*. November 1. www.theglobeandmail.com/canada/article-nearly-600-people-died-in-bc-summer-heat-wave-vast-majority-seniors/.

World Bank. 2021. "Nigeria to Improve Electricity Access and Services to Citizens." Text/HTML. February 5. www.worldbank.org/en/news/press-release/2021/02/05/nigeria-to-improve-electricity-access-and-services-to-citizens.

n.d. "Access to Electricity (% of Population)." Accessed June 6, 2022a. https://data.worldbank.org/indicator/EG.ELC.ACCS.ZS.

n.d. "Rural Population (% of Total Population)." Accessed June 9, 2022b. https://data.worldbank.org/indicator/SP.RUR.TOTL.ZS?end=2019&start=1960.

World Meteorological Organization. 2021. "WMO Recognizes New Arctic Temperature Record of 38°C." https://public.wmo.int/en/media/press-release/wmo-recognizes-new-arctic-temperature-record-of-38%E2%81%B0c.

World Resources Institute. 2021a. "Scotland: Re-Skilling through the Oil and Gas Transition Training Fund." January 4. www.wri.org/update/scotland-re-skilling-through-oil-and-gas-transition-training-fund.

2021b. "European Union's Just Transition Mechanism: Transnational Funding and Support for a Just Transition." April 1. www.wri.org/update/european-unions-just-transition-mechanism-transnational-funding-and-support-just-transition.

Young, Shalanda, Brenda Mallory, and Gina McCarthy. 2021. "The Path to Achieving Justice40." *The White House*. July 20. www.whitehouse.gov/omb/briefing-room/2021/07/20/the-path-to-achieving-justice40/.

Zaman, Rafia, Oscar van Vliet, and Alfred Posch. 2021. "Energy Access and Pandemic-Resilient Livelihoods: The Role of Solar Energy Safety Nets." *Energy Research & Social Science* 71 (January): 101805. https://doi.org/10.1016/j.erss.2020.101805.

About the Authors

Dr. Kyla Tienhaara is Canada Research Chair in Economy and Environment in the School of Environmental Studies and the Department of Global Development Studies, Queen's University. She is the author of *Green Keynesianism and the Global Financial Crisis* (Routledge 2018) and the co-editor of *The Routledge Handbook on the Green New Deal* (2022).

Dr. Tom Moerenhout is an adjunct assistant professor at Columbia University's School of International and Public Affairs (SIPA), and a resident scholar at SIPA's Center on Global Energy Policy. He also leads the energy subsidy program at Johns Hopkins' Initiative for Sustainable Energy Policy.

Vanessa Corkal is a policy advisor on Canada Energy Transitions at the International Institute for Sustainable Development. She combines her climate change expertise with over nine years of documentary, journalism, and non-profit experience.

Joachim Roth is a policy analyst with International Institute for Sustainable Development's Energy team. Joachim works on the circular economy, green fiscal policies, and coal phase-out with a particular focus on a just transition in developing and emerging economies.

Hannah Ascough is a PhD candidate in the Department of Global Development Studies at Queen's University. Her research centers on environmental charities in South Africa and internationally.

Jessica Herrera Betancur is a Master of Environmental Studies candidate at Queen's University. Her research addresses the need for worker retraining in a just transition for oil workers in Alberta.

Samantha Hussman is a Master of Environmental Studies candidate at Queen's University. Her research examines degrowth discourses during the period of the COVID-19 pandemic.

Jessica Oliver completed a Master of Environmental Studies at Queen's University in 2022. Her research focused on the role of community wind projects in the energy transition.

Kabir Shahani completed a Master of Arts in Global Development Studies at Queen's University in 2021. He now works as a research and financial analyst with the Sustainable Housing Initiative of the Rural Development Network in Alberta.

Tianna Tischbein completed a Master of Arts in Global Development Studies at Queen's University in 2021. She now works as a research analyst at the Institute of Fiscal Studies and Democracy at the University of Ottawa.

Acknowledgments

This work was supported by Mitacs through the Mitacs Accelerate Program. This research was also supported by funding from the Canada Research Chairs Program. We are immensely grateful to all of the participants who agreed to be interviewed for the research. We also appreciate the institutional support that we received from the International Institute for Sustainable Development (IISD). Finally, we would like to recognize the contribution of the anonymous peer reviewers and our editor, Aarti Gupta, who made valuable comments and suggestions for revisions to our initial manuscript.

Cambridge Elements ☰

Earth System Governance

Frank Biermann
Utrecht University

Frank Biermannis Research Professor of Global Sustainability Governance with the Copernicus Institute of Sustainable Development, Utrecht University, the Netherlands. He is the founding Chair of the Earth System Governance Project, a global transdisciplinary research network launched in 2009; and Editor-in-Chief of the new peer-reviewed journal*Earth System Governance*(Elsevier). In April 2018, he won a European Research Council Advanced Grant for a research program on the steering effects of the Sustainable Development Goals.

Aarti Gupta
Wageningen University

Aarti Gupta is Professor of Global Environmental Governance at Wageningen University, The Netherlands. She is Lead Faculty and a member of the Scientific Steering Committee of the Earth System Governance (ESG) Project and a Coordinating Lead Author of its 2018 Science and Implementation Plan. She is also principal investigator of the Dutch Research Council-funded TRANSGOV project on the Transformative Potential of Transparency in Climate Governance. She holds a PhD from Yale University in environmental studies.

Michael Mason
London School of Economics and Political Science

Michael Mason is a full professor in the Department of Geography and Environment at the London School of Economics and Political Science. At LSE he is also Director of the Middle East Centre and an Associate of the Grantham Institute on Climate Change and the Environment. Alongside his academic research on environmental politics and governance, he has advised various governments and international organisations on environmental policy issues, including the European Commission, ICRC, NATO, the UK Government (FCDO), and UNDP.

About the Series

Linked with the Earth System Governance Project, this exciting new series will provide concise but authoritative studies of the governance of complex socio-ecological systems, written by world-leading scholars. Highly interdisciplinary in scope, the series will address governance processes and institutions at all levels of decision-making, from local to global, within a planetary perspective that seeks to align current institutions and governance systems with the fundamental 21st Century challenges of global environmental change and earth system transformations.

Elements in this series will present cutting edge scientific research, while also seeking to contribute innovative transformative ideas towards better governance. A key aim of the series is to present policy-relevant research that is of interest to both academics and policy-makers working on earth system governance.More information about the Earth System Governance project can be found at: www.earthsystemgovernance.org

Cambridge Elements$^{\equiv}$

Earth System Governance

Printed in the United States
by Baker & Taylor Publisher Services